WEAPONS OF WARFARE

The Whole Armour of God

OKOROAFOR COMFORT C.

ISBN: 9789781957895

Published/Printed by:

PatUch Concepts

Email: patuchconcepts@gmail.com

+234 706 898 7100

DEDICATION

For the inspiration, support, and experiences/encounters during the process of writing this book, I dedicate this masterpiece to the Holy Spirit (my sweetheart), who has supported me on every side for the reality of this book.

Strongly, I believe that this piece (WEAPONS OF WARFARE: THE WHOLE ARMOUR OF GOD) will not just motivate Christians by touching the inheritance of the promises of God, but will also quicken the spirit, soul, and body of every believer into the mandate of a victorious walk with the Lord Jesus Christ by the Holy Spirit.

ACKNOWLEDGEMENT

I am most grateful to God Almighty for His grace and faithfulness toward me. I also acknowledge my family and friends who have always believed in me and have in diverse ways proven their love for me. God bless you all.

CONTENTS

INTRODUCTION

One of the greatest advantages we have as Christians is the assurance of God's word and his faithful promises.

The word of God is complete and trustworthy enough that we can take it as our first and last option over the situations of life and in our war against the world, ourselves, and the evil one who is the originator of all evil and who comes in different cunning ways to trick us into submitting to him instead of God.

By God's word and with the help of the Holy Spirit his plans have been exposed; therefore, where there is revelation safety resides and gains strength through God's revelation and presence to subdue him 2 Peter 1:3.

You are reading this book because you seek to inculcate in you the attitude and principles for a life full of the joy of victories, to live out God's will concerning your life; every genuine believer desires and deserves that because Christ declared us more than conquerors and that we must manifest on a daily basis.

For in that way, our Father in heaven is glorified; so therefore, I encourage you to prepare your mind, get a note beside you, and write down all the areas that are addressing your life or any situation around you, and to absorb what the

Lord is saying through this book to be empowered by His revelation to fulfil purposes.

As the title implies, WEAPONS OF WARFARE: THE WHOLE ARMOUR OF GOD, a series culled from the book of EPH 6:10-19 you'll discover the weapons you have as a child of God and how to use them effectively.

As you read, I pray God to give you enlightenment and the power (which we received through grace) to be a doer and not only a reader.

1

USE OF WEAPONS AND ARMOUR

There is a possibility that one will have something and not know how to make effective use of what he/she has, it is carelessness for one to have something and not know what he/she has. Weapons are objects or instruments for attack or defence in war/combat e.g. guns, missiles, swords, spears, etc.

These are used to inflict pain, and cause injury or damage; they can also be used for self-defence or against an enemy. Anyone who carries a weapon has the awareness that there's an enemy, therefore is prepared to contend against them anytime (Proverbs 24:10). Therefore, weapons can be used both for self-defence and for destroying.

However, since there are weapons, there is also armour; armour is primarily for protection or defence e.g. shield which is a protective metal covering that could be worn on battlefields/ battlefronts, it covers from head to feet, it can also be carried on the arm i.e. a protective structure.

2 Corinthians 10:4-6 the weapons from God to His children are not carnal; here I'm talking about spiritually enhanced weapons which are two facets i.e. it serves as a weapon

against the enemy and as an armour for the believer at the same time (PS 91:2) The word of God is the greatest weapon/armour here on earth; it is not like the one created by the greatest scientists, man-made weapons have only one usefulness – to destroy, but the one that God gives serves diverse purposes, all of which are dependent on His word. It can destroy and restore, it can tear down and build; it can overthrow and establish, it can kill and make alive; no science can produce that all in one weapon. It operates both spiritually and physically.

This weapon is completely found in the word of God which the scripture says is power; the death and resurrection of Christ granted us mortals the right to the authority of that word – to all who believe and through the Holy Spirit, the power of God is made manifest in us as sons of God.

 2 Corinthian 10:4 – The weapons we fight with are not the weapons of the world. On the contrary, they have the divine power to demolish strongholds (NIV).

Here, the truest definition and uses are stated as the divinely empowered, used for demolishing strongholds & fortresses of the adversary. This weapon is not to be used against humankind but against every satanic power manifesting itself through humans; against evil forces operating in the world against sons of men and children of God.

WHY DO WE NEED DIVINE EMPOWERED -WEAPONS?

Ephesians 6:12 says – for we wrestle not against flesh and blood, but against principalities, against powers, against the rulers of darkness of this world, against spiritual wickedness in high places (KJV).

All these adversaries mentioned in this scripture are spiritual forces but could manifest in/through the physical. People struggle or fail because they handle spiritual matters physically and emotionally instead of operating from the spiritual, and addressing the root of the issue. The devil is older than anyone on the face of the earth and can go the extra mile to achieve his wicked schemes; he understands the ways of men, while men who have the Spirit of God understand his strategies and even outrun him before his plans even take form.

He doesn't understand men of the Spirit either; men who are led by the Spirit of God are a terror to him. That's the reason we must not depend only on man's strategies but must submit to God as our source. God's wisdom is paramount to conquering him (the devil), even in his most strategic plans. Every day of our lives, we need divine intervention over all that concerns us, both spiritually and physically.

The word "divine" refers to God, not a native doctor, nor a magician, nor sorcerers, etc.; not man nor woman, but God only, (the eternal and holy one), with whom all things in heaven, Earth and underneath lie in His hands.

This adversary, who was once a servant of God, precisely an archangel, served in Heaven but rebelled against God with the act of pride exhibited, and was downcast by God. He was first the enemy of God before he became our enemy. His agenda is against all creation- to kill, steal, and destroy and more especially against believers who carry the seal of the Holy Spirit. "We became the enemies of Satan and the world the moment we became friends with Christ." And that is why we must take our stand against his wicked devices against us and all. Therefore, divine weapons are essential for our victory.

It is high time we take human abilities such as ingenuity, talents, wealth, skills, eloquence, charisma, education, and, personalities as our secondary strengths and cling to the knowledge of God through His word and the Holy Spirit - which is the only more than adequate weapon/armour capable of demolishing satanic strongholds and protecting us.

Most of these armour/weapons are listed for us in Ephesians 6: 11-19, But before we delve into that, we must understand what exactly we are fighting for and against. As explained in the preceding page, the devil is the one we are fighting against, the institute of sin, evil, wickedness, falseness, etc.

Therefore, we are fighting against unrighteousness and every scheme and knowledge of the devil.

HOW TO FIGHT VICTORIOUSLY

To fight victoriously simply means having a winner's mind-set, knowing that the greatest battle has already been won by Christ and that we see and have our victories in Him. Whoever is self–reliance can never contend victoriously, because it is only in Christ that victory is guaranteed. As the redeemed, reconciled to the Father through the blood of Christ, we must understand that - that is our first victory over Satan.

We are already on the winning team because Christ has all the power, has conquered the devil, and is glorified by the Father. He sits enthroned at the side of the Father always interceding, watching over, and advocating for all believers. Who is a believer? A believer is one who completely surrendered to the lordship of Jesus Christ as Saviour, to reverence and follow Him.

2

THE WORD

Christians are engaged in compulsory spiritual conflict with evil – the kingdom of darkness; choosing whether to fight or not is completely irrelevant because whether you like it or not – for as long as you're born of God, the fight is on, and the only option you have as a believer is to stand firm till the end, which means that you must contend for your faith and all to stand. We must always be ready, full of the word because the adversary doesn't wait for you to get ready.

This conflict is a contention for a faith that is constant until the end of the age. As earlier said, the believers' victory has been secured by Christ. Through His sacrifices, He made power available to any mortal who believed in Him, thereby rendering the devil powerless and defeated. (Matthew 12:29-30; Colossians 2:15).

Christians are presently involved in spiritual warfare by the Holy Ghost against their sinful nature/desires, against the ungodly pleasures of the world, temptations of every sort, and against Satan, and his forces; separating ourselves from the dark world system. Being soldiers of the cross, partnering with Christ both willingly and sacrificially to defend the finished work on the cross by revealing the truth and knowledge of God to the world to save many from eternal damnation, fighting the good fight of faith, living up to God's expectations in terms of righteousness, peace and, love, allowing ourselves to be vessels of honour, and revealing God and His might through us.

Therefore, for us to achieve these purposes, we must first depend wholly on God, in His strength and grace, knowing well that we can't achieve our mission here on earth just by humanistic abilities; in fact, the only way to fulfil our purpose in life is by walking with God step by step. When a man gives his heart to Christ - He comes and dwells in His fullness (John 15:7). God hears those who trust and rely on Him as their source (Romans 10:11). Having divine knowledge and understanding is vital for every believer; it transforms the soul (inner man), which manifests on the outside (physical); the word imparts divine wisdom for excellent living.

The good news of Christ brought salvation to us; and is essential to preserve us and water us to grow unceasingly inside – out, to mature into spiritual adults [Ecclesiastes 10:16-17] So, we must not forsake it because it is the foundation of our faith and for all things, including things to come.

Anyone who professes the name of Christ must live by His word, which contains His will, commands, ordinances, principles, statutes, strategies, and instructions leading to Godly ways and a victorious walk.

PROPERTIES OF GOD'S WORD:

- The word of God is TRUTH (John 17:17)
- The word of God is LIFE and SPIRIT (John 6:68, Hebrews 4:12, Philippians 2:16)
- The word of God is LIGHT (John 8:12)
- The word of God is POWER (Hebrews 4:12)
- The word of God convicts and justifies (John 16:8)
- The word of God is ALIVE and ACTIVE (Hebrews 4:12)
- The word of God in Christ Jesus etc. (John 1:1-5, 1 John 1-3). Scriptures declare that Jesus Christ is the manifold wisdom of God and perfect revelation of God's personality and nature. Just as a person's words reveal his/her mind, intention, and behaviour; so Christ (The word) reveals the personality (and nature) of God the Father.

Three characteristics of Jesus as the word are-:

1. The word's relation to the Father: Christ was self-existent with God before the creation of the world; He existed from eternity, distinct from both eternal fellowships with God the Father. Christ was divine (the word was God), having the same nature and essence as the Father (Col 2:9-10).

2. The word's relation to the world: It was through Christ that God the Father created and now sustains the world (JN 1:3, COL 1:16, Hebrews 1:2).

3. The word's relation to Humanity: "The word became flesh". In Jesus, God became a human being, having the same nature as humanity but without sin. This is the basic statement of incarnation" Christ left heaven and entered the condition of human life through the gateway of human birth". Christ was not created He is eternal.

True genuine life is embodied in Christ, His life is the light for everyone, and all God's virtue is made available to all through Him (JN 8:12). For this reason, everyone who desires to live in God's plan and purposes must come through Christ.

Nevertheless, knowing the word is not enough, it implies that you walk in the strength of His knowledge in you, not memorising the scriptures and yet in bondage; it requires that you trust and apply it in your daily living, placing a high value on it as our only means of survival and thriving

(A gift from God to us).

3

GUIDELINES FOR WALKING IN VICTORY

Ephesians 6: 10- 19 Finally, be strong in the Lord and in His mighty power (v.10, NIV). The scripture reveals the intent of God through the Apostle Paul when he admonished the Ephesian church to "be strong in the Lord and in His mighty power". We must assimilate the truth that God has given us Himself in full; it is very evident that He doesn't want us to be lonely, helpless, and stranded.

That is why, even after Christ has finished His divine assignment here on earth - He sent us the third person in the trinity (the Holy Spirit). This is the sum up of everything that pertains to Christianity or rather Godliness (2 Peter 2:2-3)

"How much we rely on God shows how well we know Him" The diversities of God that you can discover and grasp will determine the dimension in which you operate. Being strong in the Lord makes you bold instead of trembling in fear and defeat. God is not just powerful; His power is so mighty that it can do all things. If you give room for this same power to work in and through you – be ready to see the impossible happen.

Ephesians 3:20(KJV) – Now unto him that is able to do exceedingly abundantly above all that we ask or think, according to the power that worketh in us.

Now you should check yourself—which power is at work in you? Are you full of yourself, or are you filled with the Holy Ghost? Is the power at work in you divine or natural? If it is the power of God, you would certainly see, do, and exceed abundantly above too. What you have or can do should be treated as secondary when it comes to being subject to the power of God.

When a man despises God, no matter his acquirements, he has already failed [see Leviticus :26]; but God is more than able to transform the most destitute, mundane, desolate, filthy person and persons and nations to become mighty as long as there is continuous dependence on Him.

Power is an ability, capacity, vigour, strength, control, influence, authority, etc., while mighty power explains that it is beyond words, inexpressible, and unlimited. Each moment I meditate on the great love and attention we derive from

God, as feeble as we are, yet chosen by Him for wonders, filthy but justified and glorified, I get the courage to spread my wings wider and wider to soar.

Many have different things they believe or trust in, but you, child of God, where is your confidence and what is your boast? (Psalms 20: 7, Isaiah 31:1-3, AMP)

The consciousness of God will do us great good over all these things we confide in; it's a sin for a child of God to take things other than God as their hope, source, and ultimate focus in life. Trust in mortal men and material things is the reason many are frustrated in life and are living in bitterness today because they thought they had a guarantee and assurance in those things, which eventually disappointed them.

You may lose and never recover what you already have when you think you have become successful enough not to need God. Drawing strength from God preserves you from demonic influences and attacks. The scripture says, no man who believes in Him (who adheres to, and trusts in Him) will (ever) be put to shame or be disappointed [Rom 10:11; AMP].

This is a promise to encourage those who do not know Him to come closer and for those who believe to be consistent in their focus on Him. Many are giving up because of the level of opposition they encounter in life - not willing to obey God anymore like our father Abraham did, he strongly believed and trusted in God, and The Almighty was pleased with him and made his way prosperous. Romans 4:18–21(KJV).

We shouldn't entertain fear and discouragement when we have and know God. The greatest fear of every believer should be the fear of not going with God. What will become of me if I don't go with the Lord?

So therefore, committing our lives, spirit, soul, body, decisions, affairs, activities, etc.—every day is what produces results. Our Father, in all His greatness, does not look down on His people, He acknowledges and has regard for us and is always at work bringing out the best in us. I must say that God is humble, of course, we can see that in the life of Jesus, who is the express image of the Father (Hebrews 1:3), He expects us to submit to Him in love, humility, and obedience just as Christ himself did.

Being strong in the Lord is achieved by unwaveringly believing everything that comes out of His mouth; whether science has proof of it or not, whether it makes sense or not, whether people do that or not, but because it is coming from the omniscient One- we must believe it as that is the only way one can be strong in the Lord.

We mustn't have or belong to the stereotype that says God cannot do all things, even some believers think that way; for instance, when they have a headache, they believe God can cure it, but when it's hepatitis B, they are afraid, already concluding that God cannot heal it. And I command sickness to leave your body and peace to be restored in Jesus' name, Amen. Have faith in God! Act on the word!

The reason I wrote about "the word" in the preceding page is because it is something you can't do without as a believer; from there, you'd know your heritage in Christ, God's plans, will, and purpose, including His promises. You need the word to be able to face the lies of the adversary and that of the world. Your prayer and fasting will not make Satan stop making attempts against your life and destiny. Studying God's word terrifies him because his advantage against men is their ignorance, however, it still doesn't stop him from trying.

What makes him lose his mind as well as power over you is when you are a doer of what you studied from the scriptures- standing firm on God's word. When Jesus was done with fasting and prayer, the adversary found it very appealing to tempt Him, likewise, when you are fully loaded with the word, he will come to know if you are the hearer only and not the doer.

The scripture says that our adversary never rests, he roams about day and night seeking for whom he may destroy, God Himself permits certain things to come our way so that He will know how much we've grown, how much we regard Him, based on how much He has invested in you. You can see this from Job's experiences, believe me, if your eyes are opened, you'll be greatly astonished at what God does in your life daily for your spiritual and physical growth.

Jesus is our intercessor, always bearing our issues to the Father's attention; because He understands whatever is going on right in us and around us. He has gone through the same things we are going through, and something even more severe. (Hebrews 4:15-16, NIV), [Hebrews 8: 6; 7:25, 1 John 2:1-2].

Jesus is aware of how we are all feeling over issues in life, and He alone can bring a solution to them all. Remember, Christ did not come into the world as a king, but He was born into a poor home; He didn't have every one of his material needs provided for; He was also tempted, rejected, and spoken ill of by those He cared for, and many more, yet He kept the faith, never compromised in relying on the Father, was blameless before God, and was consistent in fulfilling His mandate. During those difficult days- He knew that in those very moments, He could only finish well by having God by His side.

At one time, before His arrest, He knew what was to befall Him, He became sorrowful, troubled, and deeply depressed [Matt 26:37-43] What He did was seek strength to overcome His flesh [v. 42].

I was richly inspired when I read this portion; I learned that you cannot hold onto humans, especially when life seems very tough. It was the moment that Jesus needed His friends most that they turned Him down, they couldn't stay for a watch or even pray with Him; because that was the reason He took them with Him, instead, they were all enjoying their sleep.

I thought of how Jesus felt that moment, and this thought brought me to one occasion in my home; I had a very terrible revelation that needed to be prayed for, I called on my siblings to join me for midnight prayers, but they felt disturbed and were enjoying their night rest. But all I did was face God, I prayed with all my heart to God, didn't wait any longer, and glory be to God, He answered me.

Listen, it doesn't matter how great, huge, and mighty, your challenges could be, but be rest assured that God is the mightiest, strongest, greatest, biggest, wisest, and capable of all things, so therefore, we must be strong in the Lord at all times, relying on His strength and unconditional love. When we do, He will consistently reveal Himself in and through us; and make us overcomers, blessed, and fulfilled.

Glory be to God Almighty, who gives us access to approach Him any day anytime.

4

YOUR STAND AGAINST THE DEVIL'S SCHEMES

Put on the full armour of God so that you can take your stands against the devil's schemes (Ephesians 6:11). God the Almighty already knows what we need as followers of Christ – (soldiers of the cross— to be conquerors indeed. In the beginning, Satan rebelled against God, and war broke out in heaven, and the angels that he (the devil) deceived were cast down to the earth with him. [Rev 12: 7-9].

God bestows so much glory on man and more especially on believers, the glory that was lost in the beginning was restored to us in Christ Jesus. This makes the devil furious against humanity and more furious against believers because what he was craving in desperation to share in the glory of God was given to man – to all who believe in Christ.

Believers now have the privilege of being kings and priests of God, co-heirs with Christ and heirs of God, bringing praise and glory to God. Those things that Lucifer was specially made for have been transferred to us and even more. The Bible says that the place of Lucifer and the other deceived angels was removed from heaven; they lost their place, their position, and their heritage/entitlements (Revelation 12:8). Therefore, anything he can do to drag us down to his level is what he devises to do.

John 10:10a- (KJV) The thief comes only in order to steal and kill and destroy. God knew all his strategies, and through the Apostle Paul in Ephesians 6, He revealed to us these vital principles to apply to emerge winners indeed. These instructions are not unknown to the devil, he is aware of the armour of God and wants to stop or discourage believers from utilising it. That is the essence of this book, to help you be more conscious of God and also your enemy's strategies.

You need to know your enemy to be able to overcome him. If you don't know the root cause of a problem – solving it could be frustrating. Likewise, if you don't know who God is and what you have in Christ – you may end up in defeat no matter how born again you are. Knowledge is power, and power establishes you. As we continue, you will see some of his ways and the weapons you have to win in all battles.

One thing you must watch out for on your side is that you do not open the door for the enemy yourself; Ephesians 4:27(PEV) - Don't make it easy for the devil, the boss over the bad spirits, to get you to go wrong. One of the best things we can do to help ourselves is to safeguard-putting on the full armour of God (not a few), making sure there's no space for the devil, and guarding against his robbery, destructiveness, and death (spiritual).

Sometimes, we don't do exactly as God says; it's just like when a sick person does not adhere to the prescription of a medical practitioner, he/she bears the consequences of his/her actions. God has principles, and He expects His people to be responsible too. When we follow His instructions, it gives us the right understanding of the ways of God and makes us correct witnesses to Him. God is gracious, compassionate, loving, etc. Yes, His graciousness is to produce in us power, responsibility, obedience, and victory. God is not a toy, nor is He plan less; He has it all set up for our benefit.

The complete armour is the strategy or principle by which, if applied in our daily living- we will triumph over the wicked, and we cannot jump that process. For there to be complete armour proves that we are in serious warfare. Every day of our lives we face it in different ways, which could be emotional, spiritual, or even physical.

His attacks come diversely at us, and that's the reason we must be prepared, fully ready to face him squarely. Understand this, as said earlier, we are not fighting against flesh and blood, but against spiritual forces in high places that could manifest through nature as well. We address them from the root (spiritually), and the victory manifests in the physical. Putting on the full armour of God also involves being vigilant and spiritually sensitive (having consciousness of one's spirit, soul, and body activities, including spiritual and physical manifestations) and living in godliness; godly men are a terror to darkness because the hand of God never leaves them.

If you are not godly, you are ungodly, there's no partial godliness and ungodliness. Stop calling yourself a half-Christian or a half-unbeliever because there is no such thing as half, it's either you're in or you're out. Being a mere churchgoer will not save anyone, but being Christ-like. "Go to church, hear the word, live the word, and impact the word on the world".

Christ's cross was a bridge that led us to Him and remains a bridge today, so we must contend earnestly against anything that tends to make us fall away from that path and also be a bridge where others can meet with the Lord.

Putting on the whole armour of God may seem demanding, sacrificial, self-denying, and heavy, yes, but it will keep you safe, and preserved till the end. The attacks are because of God's endowment and love upon us; we would be better off with the full armour on than without it or with just a few. The devil is incessantly angry and jealous because he has lost it all. God gave man more than what the devil was desperate for.

Therefore, the responsibility to guard our heritage using the means provided to us by the Lord is left for us to keep up with, so that we won't lose what we have to the enemy; yes, it might look heavy, but it is safer, it may look like a heavy yoke, but Jesus assured us that this will not weigh us down; rather, it will be light and easy, and the comfort and victory that come from having Him as our refuge will fill our lives.

The armour we have is divine, tested, and trusted, David trusted in this armour (which served two purposes), instead of relying on the mere man-made armour of King Saul; he stood his ground in the name of the Lord, and his enemy fell at his feet. If he had given room for fear and intimidation by his enemy (Goliath) would he have had such a glorious victory?

I give thanks to God that David did not make a mockery of himself and the entire Israelites; it would've brought a stigma on that nation entirely – the God of David and the Israelites were glorified. This is what happens when we depend on God's strategies in all our endeavours. This taught the importance of guarding our mind (as the centre of human consciousness), which influences our actions, lifestyle, imaginations, decisions, and so on.

One of the enemy's greatest strategies includes using us against ourselves. How? He roams about looking for any loophole where he could find anxiety, depression, fear, doubt, indecisiveness, low self-esteem, etc., and one thing I find helpful in living a victorious life is the ability to control/subject yourself irrespective of the facts or theories that surround the situation to what God said about you or to you – this will enable you to deal with your oppositions in a way pleasing to the Lord.

The topic of self-control must not be underestimated in Christian gatherings as it is one virtue that keeps a believer on the right track - determining against everything that could make us stumble or fall and feeding ourselves with light through healthy meditation [Colossians 3: 1-10, PHP 4:8].

Just like I learned from my experience, it was 2 years plus after the death of my mother, and everyone had moved on with life, then there came this day, I and my brother shared memories of our parents, suddenly he became emotional, I consoled, and reassured him we'll be fine, but after that moment I was lost in my thoughts I asked God questions upon questions on why He would let us become orphans, even when in my heart- the Holy Spirit was saying, "Resist this thought and believe God," I shoved it off, I was saying, "God, let's face the fact, why should you allow these things to happen?"

As this continued in my head, I became so depressed, I couldn't do anything for myself or even go out. At a time, the Holy Spirit started cautioning me, I struggled to open my mouth for prayers, I spent a week in that condition, no one knew what I was battling inside me, but as the Holy Spirit continued speaking to me, it dawned on me that I'd sinned against God; With that, in mind, I decided to seek God's face for a day.

I quietly went to the sanctuary alone, poured my heart out to God, and made peace with Him and myself. Why am I telling this story? I knew the scriptures and God's promises, and I knew the devil was attacking me through my thoughts and wishes, but I didn't respond victoriously, rather as one who was defeated by the challenges of life, if not for the Holy Spirit's intervention, this could lead to sickness or something worse. It was the day I sought the face of God that He inspired me to write this book so that other children of God will learn how to avoid or resist satanic influences.

God appeared to me and saturated me with His peace. I had left myself so vulnerable; I didn't guard my mind as I should have when I first noticed. Joyce Meyer's book, The Battlefield of the Mind, will inspire you more about how to guard your heart. Some suicide cases we hear about today are a result of the vulnerability of people's thoughts. We must learn to fight back with our minds too.

For instance, when you're sick, don't give up – tell yourself that you're healed, use the authority you have through Christ, and don't bring yourself down to where the devil wants you to be, rather, you must tell the devil where you are in faith, the place you have pictured yourself with the eyes of faith, and counter his words even though they may be supported by facts and theory.

If you strongly believe that God has already healed, you will recover quicker than expected; A woman gave a testimony on how she had an accident and was rushed to a clinic. During her stay in that clinic, a voice was reminding her of the many scars on her face and body and how ugly she looked, she almost gave into that thought, but with the knowledge of God's word and the strength of the Holy Spirit, she started confessing positively over herself. She refused to see herself in the mirror to start crying, rather, she consistently looked at the photos she took in her younger days and declared that she would be as beautiful as she was then.

As I watched her testify, there was not a single scar on her face, not even a wrinkle. She fought back, and she won. Your mind and your voice are powerful weapons and armour, use them. When you come to understand that there's nothing God cannot do, you will surely see and do wonders without limitation.

The dormancy of the mind or its inappropriate use is what instigates limitations. The Apostle Paul declared in PHP 4:13 "I can do all things through Christ who strengthens me." He saw it, believed it, and lived in it.

Colossians 2:15(KJV) - And having spoiled principalities and powers, he made a shew of them openly, triumphing over them in it. This is our confidence that we are fighting in victory, not defeat, remembering that all power in heaven, earth, and underneath belongs to our Lord. Observe, from where we read, it didn't say God will put on you His whole armour, but it says "put on the whole armour," Just as you dress yourself up each day, likewise dress yourself up with this armour, it is our responsibility to do so, being (spiritually) naked or half-dressed could attract shame or demonic harassment.

Child of God! Create no space in your life for darkness, but guard your heart with all diligence by being mindful of the things you absorb, feed on, and produce. Renewing our minds daily through healthy meditations and constantly checking up on ourselves from the inside out. Joshua

1:8(KJV). We demolish arguments and every pretension that sets itself up against the knowledge of God, and we take captive every thought to make it obedient to Christ. 2 Corinthians 10:5 (NIV)

Christian warfare connotes actively contending for our faith, and conforming to God's will. Romans 6:16 says- Do you not know that if you continually surrender yourselves to anyone to do his will, you are the slaves of him whom you obey, whether that be to sin, which leads to death, or to obedience, which leads to righteousness (right doing and right standing with God)? (AMP)

THOUGHT MANAGEMENT

1. Always remember that none of your thoughts are hidden from God (Ps 94:11a, 139:2-4).

2. Always remember that you'll give an account of every thought as well as words and deeds. (Rom 2:16; 14:12, Eccl 12:14).

3. Always remember that the mind is the battlefield – be cautious.

4. Always check if it will be pleasing to the Lord.

5. Remember that not everything that enters your mind is worth pondering.

6. Avoid those images that will later taunt your mind.

7. Remember that a thought comes from different sources, i.e., from you, from God, and from the devil, so choose wisely.

8. Be careful what you feed your soul, what your eyes see, and what you listen to.

9. Always think of what you are thinking of, and put your mind in check.

10. Be resolute in focusing your mind on Christ and heavenly things instead of earthly things (PHP 3:19, Col 3:12) for the mind controlled by the spirit is life and peace.

11. Think of how to be innovative, creative, relevant, and a blessing.

12. Study and meditate on God's word day and night.

13. Do not pay attention to falsehoods.

I call the mind the fastest traveller, but we can always revise and reverse it whenever it's going in the wrong direction.

For the rest, brethren, whatever is true, whatever is worthy of reverence and is honourable and seemly, whatever is just, whatever is pure, whatever is lovely and lovable, whatever is kind and winsome and gracious, if there is any virtue and excellence, if there's anything worthy of praise, think on and weigh and take account of these things (fix your minds on them) PHP 4:8 (AMP.)

14. Lastly, take cover against false teachers.

But I am afraid that just as Eve was deceived by the serpent's cunning, your minds may somehow be led astray from your sincere and pure devotion to Christ, 2 Corinthians 11:3 (NIV).

Paul was afraid because he saw a great increase of false teachers in the land; he knew that the only intent of these men was to beguile children of God, especially babies. At that time, the Corinthians were in danger of being deceived into accepting the distorted gospel.

Likewise, today, some masquerade themselves as sons of righteousness, whose teachings contradict the Holy Word, who have been commissioned by the devil to lure men (especially those with itching ears) away from the truth.

Therefore, we must be on guard against them, discerning through the spirit of truth, avoiding our ears from being itchy (conceited), and accepting the word abundantly in us so we can figure out their lies.

Nonetheless, we must persistently pray for those who are deceived, have backslidden, or are in personal apostasy. We must not leave an open space for the adversary in our lives individually, and we must generally protect the entire body of Christ from shame.

5

OUR STRUGGLES ARE NOT AGAINST FLESH AND BLOOD

For our struggles are not against flesh and blood, but against the rulers, against the authorities, against the powers of this dark world and against spiritual forces of evil in heavenly realms (Ephesians 6:12). Delving more into Ephesians chapter 6 (six), verse 12; it accurately describes who our opponents are and what we (as believers) struggle against. The word enemy means an antagonist, challenger, opposer, foe, rival, etc., and every human has one, whether a believer or an unbeliever, rich or poor, small or big, etc., and that enemy is called Satan.

WHO HE WAS

- He was a morning star: -This metaphor was applied to the king of Babylon, but Lucifer was referred to as the morning star. Isaiah 14:12 – How art thou fallen from heaven, o Lucifer, son of the morning! How art thou cut down to the ground, which didst weaken the nations!

- He was a covering cherub: He was one of the archangels and part of his duties was to cover the throne.
- He walked on the stones of fire: He had access to the mountain of God, God's Eden.
- He was anointed, ordained by God to serve Him.
- He was full of beauty, greatly adorned by God, and bright (see -Ezekiel 28:12-19)

HIS NATURE

We can know some of Satan's nature by knowing his name.

He is called Satan: This means an originator of evil, through him was evil inspired, he masterminds everything evil,

Devil: He is the supreme spirit of evil, ruler of demons and evil forces.

Belial: means that he is wicked, his devices are cruel, and he derives pleasure from worthless things and ungodly people.

He is the slanderer: He slandered God, turned 1/3 of the angels of heaven against God, lied to Eve against God; and is still turning men against God and themselves. The chapter of Ezekiel talked about his great merchandise and trafficking – he sells lies.

He is the tempter: this is similar to slandering, but it's more of bargaining with one's choices, desires, lifestyles, etc.; he uses the scheme called enticement and seduction to attract or deceive his victims.

The god of this age: indicates that he is the major influence on the ideals, opinions, goals, hopes, and views of the majority of the people. His influence also encompasses the world's philosophies, education, and commerce. The thoughts, ideas, speculations, and false religion of the world are under his control and have sprung from his lies and deceptions.

Satan is the prince of the power of the air; this is to signify that, in some way, he rules over the world and the people in it. This is not to say that he rules the world completely; God is still sovereign. But it does mean that God, in His infinite wisdom, has allowed Satan to operate in this world within the boundaries God has set for him. We must remember that God gave him domain over unbelievers only (2 Timothy 2:16). Believers are no longer under the rule of Satan (Colossians 1:13)

He is like a roaring lion (1 PET 5:8): The epithet roaring lion implies hunger and determination, lions roar when they are hungry, they roar to threaten and or intimidate, St. Peter is calling attention to the fact that Satan is prowling about with desire   and   determination   to   devour   sleeping sheep/shepherds; he is eyeing all Christians in turn to see which he has the best chance of.

He is the accuser of the Brethren: whenever God points out a sin, He does it gently and intentionally to stir up repentance; never to condemn or punish. God has no part in accusing. He does not keep a record of charges against us to administer punishment. He is always on our side doing all He can to clear us of Satan's accusations (Rom 8:33-34), as a Christian, if you want God to also redeem you from Satan's accusations, be sure not to accuse or condemn others whether in your thoughts or by your words and actions (John 8:3-11), when you do, you're simply taking after the devil.

Through some of his names, I'm sure you've been able to note his nature; and purpose. Therefore, when we feel hurt by our fellow humans, we should be able to view it deeper than it seems, just like Jesus said to Peter" I rebuke you Satan" He wasn't seeing Peter anymore, but he saw the devil influencing Peter to manipulate his choices and purpose.

It's high time we start understanding who the real adversary is. Truly, it is humans that allow the devil to use them, directly or indirectly, including children of God. The devil can influence you successfully if you make room for it, but when you are spiritually sensitive – you will understand his scheme as well as overcome it. Numbers Chapter. 20 revealed diverse ways Satan manipulates or influences one's actions to do the opposite of God's will.

Guarding our hearts and being conscious of our actions and responses to things, paying more attention to God's will or the Holy Spirit, will do us a lot of good, so that the enemy will not get the best of us. God knows about all the temptations that come our way, and He gives us the grace to overcome them. As He has assured us that He wouldn't let things go beyond our control, this means that; even in that temptation – He expects that we will remain in control; in control of how to receive and react.

Subjecting ourselves to the Holy Spirit helps us to be in control, which is equal to winning. One day I asked the Lord how I could overcome the temptations that surround me, how I could have peace and be happy serving God without the guilt of the approach I had taken. As I prayed, I fell into a trance, and the Lord told me, "Be like a fool."

Ignore those things that always get the best of you. Yes, you may know your right in certain things; just pretend as though you do not and move on. Yes, you may be right in certain ways; if dragging for your right often gets the best of you, allow them to win the argument.

Just be like a fool," ignore those things that always get the best of you, yes, you may know your right in certain things, just pretend as though you do not and move on; yes, you may be right in certain ways, if dragging for your right often gets the best of you- allow them to win the argument, just be like a fool. You are doing it because of me, not because you are a fool".

One thing about us humans, and especially adults, is that we like to defend ourselves, protect our reputations, stand up for our rights, and stuff like that. God gave me this counsel, which I'm sharing in this book, to help as many as I can who would want to grow above themselves and above what men perceive them to be and become what God has purposed. If we had done a lot of unserious things, maybe we wouldn't have done things that brought regrets to our hearts. We need divine wisdom to live successfully with others.

If Moses had guarded his heart on how to receive and respond to things completely, he would have been able to overcome his emotions and please God instead. No matter what we go through in life, or how we have served God, we must not let disobedience to divine instructions be our plan B.

When we obey God, even when it may not be easy- He is glorified, which is what should be our drive – to glorify God instead of trying to prove a point or glorify ourselves. God honours those who obey Him.

The bitter truth is that we can't blame the enemy for our actions, and God can't either; rather, we bear the consequences or rewards of our actions and inactions. It is also important we learn to seek God's mercy upon us, to enable us in our frailty, because He knows every challenge or temptation we face every day, even Christ Himself had his share, but He is more interested in our decisions and choices; and how we choose to handle them, whether His way or ours.

Also, one more thing we must be careful so that we don't become a stumbling block to others; we must control the way we relate and interact, honouring God in all; so that we do not make room for the devil.

Satan is not friendly to any handwork of God, believer or not; many think that Satan will love them if they serve him. When you get close to those people, you'll be shocked at the level of torment that their lives are filled with. The unfortunate thing is that people are deceived by wealth and riches, not knowing that those things are camouflaged to entice and seduce others into the same bondage of the devil.

There is no peace for the wicked, anyone who aligns with the devil is bound; their hearts desperately need liberty, but they are blinded by material things and the doctrines of the devil, and liberty is distant from such. The Devil does not love, nor does he give peace, anyone who agrees to the Devil's bargains is indirectly selling their peace, joy, and eventually their lives if they do not run to the true light.

Our enemy operates in human form; he thinks as men do, so he uses what men love and desire to attract them. That is why Scripture encourages us to renew our minds so that we can begin to think like Christ. If you have alienated yourself from God, it is time for you to make peace with Him and return to Him, He will forgive and receive you wholeheartedly, forget all your wrongs, and give you a new life that is filled with peace, joy, love, and fulfilment.

And if you're already born again, continue renewing your mind, and do not despise the Lord's corrections so that you will grow in maturity, bearing good fruits. Safety is only in Christ, but the devil will be destroyed at last, together with those who serve him.1 Thessalonians 5:22, Proverbs 29:18a.

For this purpose, if we wrestle not against flesh and blood but against principalities and spiritual forces, with our spiritual weapon, which is more than any weapon, then we are victorious. So, dear friend, deploy your weapons and fight, you are in charge, don't let the devil's arrogance weaken you, and be like David, and Goliath must fall woefully.

For this reason, we must remain grateful to God, through the blood of Christ, we are saved and made one in Christ, empowered by the Holy Spirit to continue in our victorious walk.

BENEFITS OF KNOWING YOUR PURPOSE

Next, we will look at how knowing and understanding your purpose helps you live victoriously. Firstly, what does the word purpose imply? It is the original plan of God, His initiative while forming you into existence. Now, God does not hand us our purposes at birth, as a job description would be handed to someone before or during employment; for some reason, He wants us to discover them by ourselves and grow in them.

Often, people hear and talk about purpose or destiny without truly knowing what it means. People have what they believed to be their purposes, for example –their career, profession, expertise, etc., this could be true only if there's part of God in it, not some bunch of passion to accumulate wealth and fame and power (to control others and or to do as it always suits you), but out of genuine love for God and humanity, hunger to solve problems, and to impact/change lives- In essence, any destiny that is bent only on accumulating wealth and acquiring fame without the aim of influencing things and people positively is a man-made purpose.

SIMPLE WAYS TO DISCOVER YOUR PURPOSE

- ✓ Think of that thing that creates a vacuum in your heart by not doing it.
- ✓ What is that thing that you seem to be compassionate or empathetic about when you see it, hear it, or remember it?

- ✓ What problem can you solve or things you can change not minding how much you'd have to put in or spend for it?
- ✓ What has God laid in your heart as a burden to take responsibility for?
- ✓ What do you always dream of seeing yourself do?
- ✓ Apart from being wealthy, what other things are you zealous for?
- ✓ What are those things you see others do and you genuinely wish for an opportunity to do better?
- ✓ Has God spoken to you directly, any confirmation about anything yet? Ask Him.

I expect these questions to be very helpful to you by the time you answer them with your pen and notebook in place.

Now that you know or have a clue as to what has been God's original plan for you, as a responsibility assigned to you, let's look at ways it helps you to live a victorious life. Knowledge is one virtue God endows His people with; because where there is knowledge people thrive, live in liberty, and are hard to be deceived. (See 2 Peter 1:3, Daniel 11: 32b, Proverbs 4:7).

Ignorance is deprivation and stagnation; we are instructed to seek knowledge, without knowledge, faith won't exist, without knowledge, you cannot walk in the power of God, without knowledge, you would be frustrated trying to overcome the enemy. Knowledge guides, equips, and amplifies us; it helps us be effective in all things.

Many people have a bunch of ideas about a lot of things with little or no understanding of how it works, inasmuch as knowledge is power, without a complete understanding of that which is known you may still live in error. Understanding has to do with detailing, timing, processes, pattern, etc. (Ecclesiastes 10:10). Assuming you're an electrical engineer, understanding tells you that you cannot use a lamp or zip cord wire for a microwave machine; you either use 10-, 8- or even 6-gauge wire.

Understanding gives you the ability to develop a plan B when things are failing. Understanding begets effectiveness, boosts your confidence, and makes you an expert or skilled person (Exodus 31:1-11, 38:21-23), your skilfulness speaks about your results or achievements. Even as a preacher, if you don't know how to use your time, your gifts, your resources, and your capacities, your ministry may suffer a lot of things (Titus 1:5-16).

When you read Matthew 16:21(NLT), you'll see the level at which Jesus was very plain to His disciples, informing them what would happen, where it would happen, and when and from whom it would happen. He wasn't mincing words or assuming; he was rather straight to the point.

I was in awe when I understood how precise Jesus was. Note that Jesus was not in Jerusalem when He was informing His followers, but He said that it was high time He would be going to Jerusalem, where the needful would be done. He knew the time, and he knew what to expect from the elders when He got there, He knew what their actions would result to, and He knew what would happen afterward.

It was very difficult for the devil to deceive Him through Peter's carnal words. Jesus was visionary, purposeful, focused, and ready to walk in His purpose at all costs. Look at His reaction and response to what Peter said in verses 22-23 -   But Peter took him aside and began to reprimand him for saying such things. "Heaven forbid, Lord," he said. " This will never happen to you!" Jesus turned to Peter and said, "Get away from me, Satan! You are a dangerous trap for me. You are seeing things merely from a human point of view, not from God's."

One thing you must know is that no one knows your path more than you, and not all advice is acceptable; Peter was overwhelmed by emotions on hearing what Jesus said, he suggested that Jesus shouldn't allow those things to happen, devil influenced Peter using his love for and closeness with Christ to get through, using his speech to discourage him.

Unfortunately for the devil, Jesus' heart was tightly guarded. There was no room for his operation, and He instantly resisted the devil, no time to play with His heavenly mandate. That is why you must take caution against every comfort zone and against those who love you too much so they don't become a snare against your destiny.

> ➢ Knowing your purpose enables you to make the right choices in life.
> ➢ Use your time rightly and effectively
> ➢ Develop your capacity in specific areas.
> ➢ Have the right circles
> ➢ Listen to the appropriate people
> ➢ Choose a fitting lifestyle
> ➢ Balance activities
> ➢ Makes you an opportunist and visionary
> ➢ Observe and Overcome distractions
> ➢ Pray effectively
> ➢ Being intentional and so on.

You may wonder how Jesus accurately knew His purpose, the pattern, processes, timing, and location. There's only one way, which is by constant fellowship with the Father. Jesus' life on earth has left a pattern, a footprint, that we must follow if we want to live a purposeful life. Jesus applied many patterns on His way to fulfilment which includes studying and learning from others; however, there are two that made a significant mark in His ministry. He is a man of prayer and a man of the secret place.

You can be a man of prayer and not be a man of the secret place, these two have resemblance as they involve communicating with heaven, but the different thing about the secret place is that it is a conscious or intentional spiritual affair that you choose to be connected to heaven; unlike prayer, you're only spiritually connected when you decide to pray, but Jesus, whether praying or not, His whole consciousness is glued to the Father's heart, always more intentional about hearing than speaking.

That's why the bible says that He would go to a solitary place; avoid the crowd, the noise, the activities, and even men's praise to have a heart-to-heart talk with the Father. John the Beloved practised this when he was Jesus' disciple; he would lean on His shoulder as talked, tell me, and he would hear better, and feel better. As a result of his closeness to Jesus, he received so much love and understood Christ's love. If you read the entire book he wrote- you would see how much revelation, he got about Christ and His love.

When other disciples fled for their lives including Peter who professed love for Christ, John the Beloved never left; when Jesus was giving up the ghost, it was to this same John that he handed his mother Mary; after Jesus' ascension, John was the one chosen to carry the revelation of Christ, and of things to come to the body of Christ.

Christ specifically handed things that were important to Him to John, because obviously, He knew John and they understand each other- that is what the secret place does, it changes a man and presents him to be more favoured by God. The same thing about David – he spent time alone with God in the bush, praising God with a harp, singing heartfelt songs to God, and appreciating the wonders of His creation.

The more he did this- the more of God's attention he got until he became a man after God's heart, a man who knows God and His ways, professing how much he loved His precept. Prayer connects you and things around you to God, in other words, you address things going on around you in place of prayer. Many people, including believers, are living their lives in assumption; they don't have any focus in regards to God's will for them; they live on the suggestions and opinions of others, they don't have direction, and they're tossed about front and back.

My request to God daily is to always live my life, and make my choices and decisions under the influence of His Light (Acts 4:28) I was formed by Him and therefore need Him to lead me according to His purpose, don't wish for options outside Him.

There's a reason you were born where you were born, a member of that family, and a citizen of that country and so forth; there's no coincident in destiny, and how you handle your today will determine where and who you'll be tomorrow; For as a man would, before building a house, draw the plan of the house, so the creator drew the life plan of every human on the surface of the earth and designed beforehand how it would be, that is, faith; seeing ourselves in God's eyes and word; this is the drive and force that will push and move us to truly live up to what we are made of.

When you live in fear and intimidation, it means that you don't see the specialty of God in us, the value He placed in us; you only see yourselves through your own eyes or as others perceive. Do you know that, if you see yourself as God does, your success and achievement become just a sign, but you continue to move like Abraham, who looked for a house that wasn't made by man even after God blessed him on all sides?

In the old covenant times and until the new covenant times, God, in His infinite kindness, has always instructed men and women according to His purposes, people like Gideon, Nehemiah, Moses, Samuel, Daniel, Esther, Mary and Joseph, Paul, the 12 disciples, and many more; likewise, God is still leading people to their destinies today.

However, as you know God's plan for you, another thing is being able to walk in it. Knowing is important but not enough because there are forces that contend against the rise of men. There are some qualities you need to develop in yourself intentionally to not throw in the towel, I'll list some of them out, and they include:

Resilience – Mary was resilient in raising Jesus according to the instructions she received, unbending in times of opposition. How much or how far we can stand for God and on His words shows how our lives depend on Him. And that God guides you doesn't mean there would be no opposition, when the storm rises even against our obedience, look unto heaven and He'll show up.

Persistence- this virtue helps us to overcome the challenge that comes with failure; when people fail, they intend to give up and not try again; but if you're persistent you won't give in to discouragements and failure. It entails speaking life to that which seems dead and hopes to hopelessness.

Courage and boldness - are a product of faith that empowers you to stand against mountains and giants obstructing your way physically or spiritually.

Forbearance- this implies patience; and self-control, many people did not fulfil their purposes because of a negative approach to their desperation and appetite. Patience and control over oneself will save us a lot of deals.

Diligence and decisiveness – these overpower procrastination, ensure progress in productivity, and prove the law of consistency.

Time management – setting your time- bound goals and working with them. The temptation to lose focus is high, but when you set your daily targets and priorities, you'll win. Being a person of pen and note enables you to be on track, gives you a clearer picture of things, and the ability to refer back when forgotten.

Be teachable- seek knowledge, and don't settle for less, what you know gives you an edge in life or a place among men. Seek God, His words, His secret place, His presence, etc. - there you'll draw strength to pursue.

When you build your capacity, you're on your way to glory. You don't just sit down and do nothing and expect destiny to happen. Opportunity happens by time and chance; destiny meets those who are ready; and your destiny finds you when you have built up or are building up constantly on your potentiality. Working and investing in yourself is a way of placing an order from heaven and earthly realms concerning yourself; it shows your readiness, which will eventually be found by an opportunity call from heaven and earth.

Every destiny has eternal value, e.g., Paul's destiny was to work for the kingdom of God; he paid immeasurable prizes for the Gospel of Christ and the souls of men; the only joy he possibly had must've been his fellowship with Christ and the reward of his labour which surpasses the pain he went through, make sure it's God's purpose, not your mere desire, every destiny has a cost too, there are certain things you'd have to deny yourself of; or starve some passion that kills destinies. The good news is that whatever you sacrificed will return to you bigger and better.

As our faces are different, so are our purposes, don't copy anyone, seek and do yourself only, like Jesus himself, He said that His meat (food i.e. desire and overall goal) is to do the will of the one who sent Him(paraphrased) this was when others were concerned about food (John 4:31-34) and also Mary the sister of Lazarus, Martha chose to serve the table while she (Mary) chose to listen to Jesus' teaching (Luke 10:40-42).

Don't let the devil keep you busy with what may seem to be camouflage; don't just be busy for sake or walk in men's opinions. Emulate Christ, who was very conversant with His assignment, and so He did not give in to any form of deceit-Matthew 4:1-11, Jesus overcame the enticement of the devil; when you know your purpose, you'll be able to recognize the devil's attack on it - Mark 8:27-33.

He knew that the enemy wanted to use another means to discourage His spirit; he turned back, looked at the rest of His disciples, and quickly rebuked Satan. When I came across this portion, I asked the Lord why Jesus had to look at His disciples and what happened. He said it was because He wanted to call back His consciousness, He was reminding Himself of the purpose for His coming to the world, He needed to look at the faces of those whom He has come to save and make a difference in their lives.

He recalled that if He gives up, these people He loves as family and friends will suffer endlessly. Jesus knew that he had to finish his assignment in order to achieve the purpose of God for mankind. He was very discerning and sensitive to everything. Jesus is the word that surpasses every other word, he has excellent wisdom and understanding; and is slow to speak, He patiently weighs his reactions, He is the word that became flesh – therefore, no word of man or devil could make Him fail.

Your meat must not be what people suggest to you, nor let it be your mere human desire- rather, let it be that which God has instructed on.

As God has helped me and is still helping me to grow in living His word, when my life wasn't in order and I was burdened with the hunger to please the Lord, to work consciously on my spiritual health and moral ways, anyone who would hear me pray would wonder if I didn't have other needs because all I asked God for was more of what is not materialistic; God showed me mercy, He spoke to me on how to overcome my struggles, fears, and challenges.

I'll be sharing those two points here because there is a heavyweight the enemy places on us and we also place on ourselves that doesn't allow us to move. It will help you to be intentional about winning self and the devil,

MATURITY- It's a result of following the Lord's command; if you want to overcome sin- you must allow the Holy Spirit to produce in you- maturity. Fruits that are always ripe for the master's use. Submit your thoughts and emotions to the Holy Spirit's voice or urges and you will not do as you wish,

I'm repeating this here for emphasis, He said "BE A FOOL" pretend not to see or hear certain things that provoke you to act unlikely. Forget things that could get to you when you remember them, BE FREE! Hold no grudge, bitterness, or unforgiveness, talk mildly, and let them cheat you or sit on your right, that's what it may seem like, but just a mere mirage.

God is not pleased with the church that professes Christ on the lips without His fire in their hearts. Don't neglect how furious God feels when His people are idolaters and disobedient to Him. Grace can help you when you don't ignore it and seek it with the right hunger – it works and supplies strength to you.

Apostle Paul asked, "Are we to continue in sin that grace may abound?" God forbid, he said. I always tell myself and others that asking for mercy implies genuine repentance of your sins, asking Him for mercy, and beginning to live a new life in Christ. Then you'll see the joy unspeakable in your life because, when you surrender to Christ, the kingdom of God is established in you. Praise God!

The Devil is very crafty (cunning) in his doings, he knows the hunger and needs of men and therefore uses it against them. That's why we must put away flesh, crucify the flesh daily, starve the flesh daily, and be filled with the Holy passions, love and righteousness, walking daily in and with the Holy Spirit. Zachariah 4:6.

You mustn't give in to desperation, because it brings about confusion and leads to error. Whatever you desire or need, confidently hand it to God and also allow Him to always guide your choices and decisions, your heart, and everything that concerns you.

James chapter 4:7 says- Submit yourselves to God. Resist the devil, and he will flee from you (NIV). To submit means – yielding to authority or paying allegiance to authority. The Almighty requires of everyone, great and small, poor and rich, leaders and followers, man or woman. The maker of the universe points out to men the need to surrender to His lordship, and revere Him.

When we live like this, we automatically become a threat to the enemy. When we open our mouths and resist him, he'll flee from us in seven directions, Hallelujah! The reverse is the case too, i.e., when one is not paying allegiance to God, the devil will come with his cohorts and dwell with the fellow. No one can serve two masters at a time; either you obey this or you disobey that, and whoever you allow in your life comes in its fullness.

When God is in charge, the Trinity dwells within us, with the fruit of the spirit manifesting in and through us with blessings overflowing; the same is true with Satan; he comes with his demons and evil forces, and he'll plant thorns of pain, sorrow, bareness, and all sorts of evil manifesting in your life and through you as well.

Nothing good comes from him, he is full of deceit. Therefore, we must test every spirit because Satan's agents are everywhere seeking to deceive people. May the Lord release on you the spirit of discernment in Jesus' name, Amen!

2 Corinthians chapter 11:14- and no wonder, for Satan himself masquerades as an angel of light. No child of God does not carry the spirit of God in Him. The Holy Spirit is the seal God places on His people as a symbol of ownership through salvation. Anyone without this spirit is living outside the kingdom of God. Just as Christ was conceived by the Holy Spirit, so shall every child of God; His spirit possesses our spirit man to bring the perfection of God the Father into His sons.

This same Holy Spirit is our teacher, comforter, helper, guardian, etc. He releases diversified gifts into us, which make us manifest His presence as well as do extraordinary things. One of the virtues He fills us with is the spirit of wisdom, i.e., the ability and power to understand, know, discern, and reason, beyond what is seen and beyond natural men; with the spirit of wisdom, one can be able to distinguish between God and the ungodly.

The Holy Spirit Himself reveals secret things from God to us. Anyone without Him is totally in darkness and is also spiritually blind. According to what we read, it says that he camouflages himself as light while his true nature is darkness. This portion calls for a steady awareness of the activities that happen around us and paying attention to every detail in our affairs with other fellows.

However, we must persistently maintain His (the Holy Spirit's) presence. How can one maintain the Holy Spirit's presence? By being truthful to yourself and to God, by putting yourself on the balance of God's word, by aligning your soul's activities (mind, thoughts, imagination, desire) to the truth, and by keeping our body (God's temple) clean (1 Thessalonians 5:23; Rom 12:1).

Therefore, when you are at peace with your maker, He will open both your heart and eyes to see every appearance of evil and how to overcome it. This gift of discernment is necessary for every man, but it is especially important for believers, so that we may not fall into the pit of deceit. One thing is hearing or receiving revelation from God, while another is utilising it.

We mustn't be stiff-necked to God's voice, nor even try to weigh how factual or scientifically proven it may be or sound, because the mind, thoughts, and ways of God are farther than ours. (Isaiah 55:8-9). Our minds grow when we cultivate the pattern of trusting God in all things, knowing that He is faithful to keep and do all we commit to Him.

The mistake people make is using their humanistic wisdom to access the spiritual; God is bigger than man's philosophy and traditions and is beyond our facts. People who depend solely on facts don't live above them, they don't understand the supernatural, and this was what made Abraham unique. He never doubted or figured out God's word carnally; rather, everything he heard from God he simply obeyed. That's the kind of faith God is seeking from His sons today.

6

THE FULL ARMOUR OF GOD

Therefore, put on the full armour of god, so that when the day of evil comes, you may be very able to stand your ground; and after you have done everything, to stand. (Ephesians 6:13)

God, I always say, is not a magician, neither does He show favouritism (1 Peter 1: 17; 2 Chronicles 19:7). He has standards, and principles; just as a sick person consults a medical practitioner for medical advice/direction (for his/her wellbeing), so should everyone who has believed in Christ and wants to finish well is expected to follow with all humility the precepts of God.

Putting on the whole armour of God as listed in the scripture helps in covering our frailty and vulnerability (spiritual nakedness and bankruptcy) to the enemy or things that could destroy us. Earnestly living up to God's expectations is the criterion for a victorious life over the adversary.

God has prescribed to us as our Lord in Ephesians 6:13 to put on His armour in its full measure to enjoy its advantages in full measure too. The armour of God as stated in the preceding page, is for our protection on the war fronts/battlefields. This armour could be physically invisible but spiritually visible, though the results of its activity reflect both the physical and the spiritual. Even the enemy can distinguish between those that are putting it on and those that aren't. The armour of God is indestructible and infallible; it was specially made by God Himself, for His people.

For one to have this armour/weapon it requires first having knowledge of the maker and being in a relationship with Him. The armour of God cannot be acquired by wealth, connection, through trade by barter, or academic qualifications; but by "being" a kingdom citizen and a God lover (Acts 19:11-16).

Today, many think that they can acquire God's abilities through their possessions. God's power can only be given from one source and can be received through one process, which is by believing in Him and being in right standing with God (living up to His expectations in humility and obedience}. ACTS 8:18-22.

The only reliable and right source of God's power is the Holy Ghost, which He generates in us through the word of God that we listen to, read, and absorb; He brings the word of God alive in us, which in turn produces extraordinary power in our spirit, which also manifests in the physical. Anyone who thinks they can get the power of God for free is deluded.

Such a fellow has been blinded by his thoughts, evil desires, and motives. Such thought cannot emanate from any other source than the devil, and it is known for its selfish and evil motives.

This is one of the reasons children of God must be careful with their thoughts or motives in which they do the things they do because every man's work will be tested, everyone's motive for serving in God's vineyard will be seen, and everyone will be rewarded according to their labour (2 Corinthians 5:10-11}. Now, there is some set of people who would not be delighted to talk less of witnessing the white throne judgement. {Rev 7:1-3} These are those who bear not the seal of God upon them.

Therefore, in essence, we must, with all focus, adhere to the principles of God so that we may be victorious and acquire the seal He gives, which guarantees us as those who have overcome permanently/eternally.

Nevertheless, now that we are working towards our eternal salvation, we ought to remember and go along with our work tool which is the whole armour of God. Our maker is rightly aware that the day of evil will come; even Jesus confirmed that each day has enough trouble of its own (Matthew 6:34). that's the reason we need the whole armour of God on us every day of our lives, not sparing anyone.

 In John 15:4-11, Jesus emphasised on abiding in Him, as He is the vine and we (The Redeemed) are the branches. The understanding that we cannot do without the vine should be imbibed in us; just as a branch withers when it is cut off from the tree, or as a tree withers when it is uprooted, so is anyone who is disconnected from Christ {the source}; a such person becomes fruitless or would suffer loss, and if care is not taken such person could be used for firewood. The source of every man is God the creator of Heaven and Earth {Ps 24:1}.

When we are connected or joined with Christ {as the vine}, he releases on us the essential virtues that keep us alive, fruitful, and nourished, both spiritually, physically, and mentally. Bearing fruit which is one of God's wills for His children cannot still be achieved outside Him.

Psalm 91:1, 9-10 says-1 He who dwells in the shelter of the Most High will rest in the shadow of the Almighty. If you make the Most High your dwelling, even the Lord who is my refuge. Then no harm will befall you, no disaster will come near your tent.

The assurance of safety is that when we dwell in the presence of God, seeking Him for ourselves, loving Him, abiding in Him, and delighting in His word, then we have all we need to stand. From our text in Ephesians 6:13, the B part of it says "after you have done everything to stand".

Reaching that height that God recognizes as standing is the everyday pursuit of the lovers of God and righteousness, those who walk in the consciousness of His kingdom, surrendering their hearts to obedience - His dos and don'ts— not necessarily bound by the law or thoughts of sin, but allowing themselves to be different in the way that pleases God, with His word engraved on the board of our hearts, keeping ourselves in check all the time.

To stand is a big responsibility, but everyone who believes in Jesus sees it as worth doing because of the great love and sacrifice that have already been put out for us. That is why the Bible says that 'he that is forgiven much loves much' (Luke 7:47 paraphrased), and your willingness to obey, to stand for Christ is proof that you love Him without reserve.

Matthew 5:6 says- Blessed are those who hunger and thirst after righteousness: for they shall be filled. This is one of the most important verses in the Sermon on the Mount. The ability to stand depends on the level of thirst and hunger in you, everyone's hunger and thirst are not all the same, even though we are all believers. And this hunger and thirst increase the more we know God, as we also relate to or fellowship with Him on different levels. Such hunger is seen in Moses {Exodus 33:13, 18}, the psalmist {Ps 42:2, 6 & 63:1} and apostle Paul {PHP 3; 10} etc. The spiritual condition of Christians throughout their lives will depend on their hunger and thirst for;

- The presence of God (Deuteronomy 4:29)
- The word of God (Psalm 119)
- The Communion of Christ (Philippians 3:8-10)
- The fellowship of the Spirit (John 7:37-39, 2 Corinthians 13:14)
- Righteousness (Matthew 5:6)
- Kingdom power (Matthew 6:33) and
- The return of the Lord (2 Timothy 4:8)

Christians' hunger for things of God is destroyed by worldly anxiety, the deceitfulness of wealth (Matthew 13:22), desire for things (Mark 4:19), life's pleasure (Luke 8:14) and failure to remain in Christ (John 15:4). When the hunger of believers for God and His righteousness is destroyed, believers die spiritually.

After a person believes in Christ and is forgiven, he or she receives eternal life and the power to remain in Christ. Given that power, the believer must then accept that responsibility for salvation and remain in Christ. The conditions by which we remain in Christ are by keeping God's word in our hearts and minds and making it the guide for our actions, drawing our strength from Christ, obeying His commands, remaining in His love, loving each other, keeping our lives clean through the word, resisting all sin, and yielding to the Spirit's direction.

Every believer should be able to pray as David did in PS 63:1. It describes a man's deep longing in the heart for God, one that can only be satisfied by an intimate relationship with Him. Those who profess to know God should examine themselves by asking the following:

1. Do I possess a strong desire for God and His presence in my life?

2. Do I go through life largely consumed with secular pursuits and worldly entertainment, while prayer, Bible reading, and a deep hunger and thirst for God and His righteousness have little place or vitality in my life?

For this reason, we must be sensitive to the Holy Spirit's convicting work in our lives. Every child of God must put on complete armour, so that you may be able to resist and stand your ground in the day of evil, having done all the crisis demands or requirements of God, to stand firmly in your place.

2 Corinthians 10:6 says- And we will be ready to punish every act of disobedience, once your obedience is complete (NIV). The word complete is the expectation of God towards His people, He wants perfection, wholesomeness, and orderliness of the spirit, soul, and body. This completion is achieved by paying allegiance to God in all aspects of life, not by self-righteousness (which makes it a burden) but by the Spirit (who makes it lighter).

The place we read is simply saying that we must first obey God for us to be able to stand; you cannot be lying down and think you can save another person that's in the pit, you cannot be disobeying God and think you'll become somebody (as He has proposed) in life. You cannot live in darkness and intend to shine as a light.

God cannot be deceived and does not show favouritism. Many people today have left the log of wood in their eyes, but pointing at the tiny dust in another's (can you even see?); our obedience first must be complete before we teach others how to obey.

I remember a vision when I saw the Lord, He was holding a manuscript in His hand, and He read it out to me saying "Be Holy, for I am Holy". Meanwhile, to me, I was doing well at least; then I had to call myself back on the check because God cannot lie and He's always right about everything and I desire to live up to His expectations.

After you've done everything that is in obedience to God, you can stand to resist, fight, and rebuke the devil and he will flee from you. When you are not in right standing with God, the devil will treat you like he did to Simon the sorcerer {Acts 8:18-22}; but if yes you are in right standing with God, when you call Him He'll say here I am. (Isaiah 58:9).

The scripture teaches that no believer who is indwelt by the Holy Spirit can be demon-possessed; the spirit of God and darkness can never take part in or dwell in the same body. Demons, however, may influence the thoughts, actions, and emotions of Christians (Matthew 16:23} who fail to heed the Holy Spirit's leading {because we have free will to make every choice we want and at the same time take responsibility for them all. Christ bestows authority on His followers, (Mark 16:17-18; Luke 10:17-19) so that in boldness and confidence they may confront and overcome the devil and his cohorts; subduing the power that he wants to exert over us and others by the strength of the Holy Spirit.

Mark 3:27- No one can enter a strong man's house and carry off his possessions unless he first ties up the strong man. Then he can rob his house (NIV).

The spiritual conflict against Satan involves:

i. Declaring war against Satan according to God's purpose

ii. Entering Satan's house (any place where he has a stronghold), overpowering him by prayer and proclamation of the word, and destroying his weapon of demonic deception and temptation.

iii. Carrying off his possessions, i.e. setting free those who have been held captive by Satan's power and giving them over to God so that they may receive forgiveness and sanctification through faith in Christ.

The following are the individual steps we should take in this process:

i. Recognize that we are in conflict against spiritual forces and powers of evil, not against flesh and blood.

ii. Live before God, fervently committed to His truth and righteousness.

iii. Have faith that Satan's power can be broken in any specific area of his domain, and realize that believers have powerful spiritual weapons given by God for the destruction of Satan's strongholds.

iv. Proclaim the Gospel of the kingdom in the fullness of the Holy Spirit.

v. Suppress Satan's power by believing in Jesus' name, using God's word, praying in the spirit, with fasting, and driving out demons.

vi. Pray especially for the Holy Spirit to convict the lost concerning sin, righteousness, and judgement.

vii. Pray for and eagerly desire the manifestation of the Spirit through the gift of healing, tongues, miracles, signs and wonders.

viii. Above all, seek obedience to God, and then you can stand as His instrument. Standing is not merely standing on your feet; it is being in right standing with God, standing out for God, and making a difference according to God's purpose. Just like what we read in Mark 3:27 before the devil can overpower a man, he will first bring in fear or timidity, depression, weakness, slumbering, and the like.

His first attack would be to make your spirit man inactive, and when this happens, he could overpower you at that moment until you decide to rise. We mustn't allow spiritual weakness to set in, that's why the Scripture encourages us to be sober and vigilant like soldiers.

I got this rhema, and I learned that we were made in place of the fallen Lucifer. When God cast Satan down, he (Satan) probably was bragging about how unique his worship service is to God "Who brings you glory as I do? Who would praise you like me? Who will exalt you? Do you think you can do without me?

Do you think you would attract such great honour if not for the huge part I play" oh yes! I see a lot of proud talk going on here; he lifted up his heart against God, desiring to share the glory of God (Ezekiel 28:13-19); then God said "Son of disobedience (Satan), today you will know that I alone am God, and I can do all things; the glory I will not share with any, and I alone will reign, my praise and glory lasts forever.

I am the creator that was not created, the all-doing one who uses the foolish things to confound the wise and the proud; He moulded with the dust, breathed His breath into His sculptor and He called it Man, which is you and I, so that we may bring praise and glory to his name to disgrace Satan the more. So tell me why the devil will not fight you, beloved. He made us so precious and enviable; He made us in His image and likeness, and He still gave us authority, power, and dominion over all things, including Satan. PRAISE GOD! That's the reason we must not be like Satan, like children of disobedience dishonouring God, but as children of righteousness (not negotiating with evil, resisting him in all senses) so that our adversary will not ensnare and torture us at last.

If you read the account of Job in Job 1:1, 1:6-12; 2:1-6, many will be wondering how the devil still communicates with God if he has been banished from heaven; yes, before Christ's death and resurrection, Satan had occasional access to God's presence, whereby he could question the sincerity and righteousness of a believer {Job).

However, nowhere in the Bible does it say Satan has direct access to God under the new covenant. Though he still aims his accusations at believers, we may overcome this accusation by Christ's blood, a good conscience, and the word of God. We can be further encouraged by the fact that we have an advocate with the Father- Jesus Christ, who is at His right hand interceding for us (Hebrews 7:25, 1 John 2:1).

Nonetheless, Job was a great icon; throughout his time of trial he didn't rub mud on the name of the Lord. God knew quite well that His servant would not disappoint Him, and God was even more proud of him. This should indeed serve as a lesson to us Christians when a man honours God- God honours him in turn.

7

THE BELT OF TRUTH

Stand firm then, with the belt of truth buckled round your waist, with the breastplate of righteousness in place (Ephesians 6:14). In those days, a belt was called a girdle; this girdle is a cord or strip of cloth worn around the waist. They use it to tighten their clothing in order to stay fit.

It shows readiness. It is also used for girding up a loincloth, which was mostly worn in those days. Loincloth is a long piece of cloth, passed between the thighs and wound around the waist; it is a one-piece garment, mostly kept in place by a belt, and it covers the genitals. Having explained what a belt is and its uses both now and in old times, let's take a look at what Paul meant by "the belt of truth".

The belt he spoke about here is no longer the physical one that is attached to their outfit, but, just like Jesus, he used physical things to point to unseen things so that we could understand them. E.g., when He was trying to let the disciples know what He was commissioning them to do, instead of saying, 'I will make you catchers of men' He said, ' I will make you fishers of men, he uses terms we can relate to – to give us a clearer picture of the spiritual things, and time to ponder on it.

The belt of truth is the spiritual girdle that holds you, the truth of God that sustains your soul, purges you, makes you free, and establishes you in Christ; it is your conviction about God and His word. It is not your opinion or facts, you hold your opinion, but your conviction holds you beyond facts and opinion, the tradition of men, philosophy, secures other pieces of armour in place. The belt of truth keeps you fit for an extraordinary walk with God.

Studying the word and spiritual patterns are ways to gain divine approval; it fills you with power, faith, and understanding. Divine approval means that God will use you mightily and can entrust to you, things that are important and valuable to Him. 2 Timothy 2:15, Acts 2:22.

The more of His truth you have, the more powerful and supernatural things you will do. The truth shapes your perspective, sharpens you into the fashion of God, and graces you to bend to the divine leading because having the word in you is having His life as long as your faith is founded upon it.

I Kings 18:46 – "And the hand of the Lord was on Elijah; and he girded up his loins, and ran before Ahab to the entrance of Jezreel." Many times in the scripture, God commands "Gird up your loins", because it is a symbol of fitness or readiness for God's power to be manifested.

If Elijah had not tucked his cloak in and girded it, he wouldn't have run as fast as he did, despite the fact that it was by the power of God. God uses every man according to how much knowledge of Him we have. Elijah was a man of faith; during his ministry days- he manifested so much fierceness and wonders that had not existed because he knew and believed God. We gain God's approval by the measure of truth in us and how we operate/walk with his truth.

Therefore, we limit ourselves when we don't have enough of it because God's approval or power operates on believers according to their spiritual maturity, which happens not by just being born again, but by devoting themselves to knowing God and His patterns. When you love the truth, the mantle is automatically released on you.

The belt of truth here also signifies your covenant with God, which usually has requirements or expectations attached from both sides. Walking in His word is the same as keeping His covenant, and when we do, He pours out His blessings.

More so, this belt of truth is not solely meant for pastors and bishops, etc.; rather, it is for every child of God, so, every form of lackadaisical attitude ought to be put out to avoid making a shipwreck of your life and the purpose of God concerning you.

Beloved, gird up your loins so that you will not disappoint your maker, including those of whom your light is meant to shine here on earth; so that your nakedness and your weakness will be covered against mockery and demonic activities; so that you can run swiftly without hearing the voice of condemnation and accusation (John 4:23-24, Romans 8:1) fortify yourself with strength and power, let the belt of truth uphold you. See Jeremiah.1:17.

Girding up our loins is not optional for believers, but a piece of advice or instruction that is coming from a loving and concerned Father who knows quite well what His people would go through as pilgrims.

Joshua is one example of those who knew the importance of God's word in everything, he invested his time to hear it and draw strength from it. [Trusted in God's word] What amazes me is the level of confidence Joshua put in every word God spoke to him and the way he kept on and on confessing them.

In Joshua 1:1-9, God gave Joshua a task to accomplish, directions on how to fulfil his assignment, promises that he'd always look up to, and warnings and instructions that would guarantee his success if heed to; Joshua held onto these words firmly and succeeded in that assignment.

Again the Lord gave him another task in Joshua 8:1 to war against Ai; with the same words He spoke initially; and he continued victoriously, and he waxed stronger and stronger because he built his world on the word of God; Joshua believed and confessed the word of God in chapter 10:25, and it became more realistic in his life.

Being able to speak God's word over a difficult situation is proof that you treasure, believe, and depend on it, knowing that what God says is the truth, and His promises are real. Luke chapter 6:46-49 distinguishes between those who have built their world upon God's solid rock and those who thought it irrelevant

Remember, building a house on a rock is never easy, people that live in rocky places can attest to this. Notice, Jesus didn't say the wind, flood, or torrents won't come because he built his house on the rock. Obedience to God is not gender based; rather, it is the heartbeat of those who have reverence for God. Doing the will of God in this perverse age requires a lot of spiritual strength and maturity.

It becomes a burden when you are self-dependent. The rock by which we build our houses (spirit, soul and body) is Jesus Himself (the Word); that was the reason I took time in the preceding pages to expatiate the functions of the word. Without the word you are empty; your life can never make any sense without Him.

You must allow the word to be rooted in you by aligning your life to the Holy Spirit's activities because He is the one that builds, not you; your flexibility to the Holy Spirit makes a solid you. Naturally, you have no power to overcome the enemy, but the Spirit of God keeps you vigilant, girded, and prepared, which will bring God glory.

God always comes through for His people, He is always willing and ready to support us, and still, He loves to see our efforts, passion, and desires, because it matters so much to Him. The level of your zeal can move God to do unimaginable things for you and even for a nation.

Refuse to give into falsehood, deceit, and camouflage, some facts are irrelevant, if you depend on them- they will end up keeping you stagnated. Do not allow the thorns and briers of life to choke the word of life in you because that's all you've got, protect it with all diligence, always meditate on it, confess it, and be hopeful in it.

Luke 8:11-15 explained the parable of the sower and what the seed represents – the word. Always believe in the words or promises of God like Ezekiel 28:24 – No longer will the people of Israel have malicious neighbours who are painful briers and sharp thorns. Then they will know that I am the Sovereign Lord.

Always put your name in those places where names are mentioned, if you claim it- it will manifest in your life, Praise

God! Let the word of God always keep you ready, let it be your action point in life. David was a typical example; he had always sought God's directions before engaging in any battle; when God says "go" he goes, when He says "stay," he stays; the words and promises of God were technically his belt of truth.

Many today are using substitutes in place of the truth; they have girded themselves with alternatives other than the truth, such as philosophies, empty deceit, principles of the world, and doctrines of men and traditions that lead to bondage and destruction. However, if you are in such a situation; do yourself a whole lot of good by seeking and clinging to the truth so that you might be free, because anyone ignorant of the truth is under serious satanic influence and bondage.

Being wealthy and learned doesn't point out that one's life is endearing to God, but walking with God does. Jesus is the only way, the truth, and the life; no one comes to God the Father except through Him. If you don't know Him- you don't know the Father, and if you refuse to know Him- the Father will not recognize you. Don't deceive yourself by saying, "I know God but I don't know Jesus," (as some are fond of saying); turn now, seek Him and you will find Him for He promised so.

How do you seek to know Him? How well do you know Jesus? You can know Him personally not only by searching the scriptures but also by communicating with Him. Some people today are living their lives without knowing it; they don't know what they are practising, and they only answer the name "Christian. " They know it's good to be or do good, but they don't know who they supposedly ought to imitate, they are more interested in laws and doctrine but are very far from the one who instituted those laws and doctrine.

The scripture states that Cornelius was a God-fearing man, who gave alms to people, and prayed continually (literally, he does well); God saw his zeal and was moved to enlighten and redirect him appropriately through Peter (Acts 10).

Likewise, some people's zeal is not properly aligned because they've not delved into a deeper knowledge of the Master in person, there is a vacuum in them despite all the good things they do because the very important and most essential thing is missing —the revelation of God through personal discoveries that are available through seeking God mostly privately. So, the belt of truth and the breastplate of righteousness are obtained when one is engrafted in Christ. The evidence of aligning with Christ is a transformed life {1 Peter 1:14-15}.

Righteousness is living God's life and/or God living in and through you. This brings us to the breastplate of righteousness. Many times we talk about the heart; it could imply the mind or soul as the centre of our being; therefore, it is very delicate and needs careful handling and security.

Proverbs 4:23[NLT] – "Guard your heart above all else, for it determines the course of your life". This piece of armour is to protect your mind against unhealthy thoughts, desires, imaginations, etc. that flow from within and from other harmful and destructive things that are thrown at you consciously or inadvertently, things that you do not have control over or get to choose. For instance, you don't get to select what you see or hear all the time, but putting on the breastplate of righteousness implies that you get to decide how those things you see or hear affect your life, choices, and lifestyle. It is the ability to be in control of your thoughts and all the things that spring from within you.

Being intentional and able to check your emotions, imaginations, thoughts, etc. so as not to cross the boundary, anything that crosses the boundary could be very extreme or ungodly, and that endangers your daily function, your life, and ultimately your soul. The breastplate of righteousness serves as a watchman of the mind, it flashes the torch to help you see, nonetheless, it is not automatic, meaning that we must use it consciously; the Holy Spirit helps us to activate its efficacy.

Psalm 119:9, 11[AMP] – How can a young man keep his way pure? By keeping watch (on himself) according to your word (conforming his life to your precepts). Your word I have treasured and stored in my heart, that I may not sin against you.

The heart of righteousness means that you have the word of God flowing in your heart, testing every thought and desire that passes by in the eyes of the scripture. The breastplate of righteousness cannot be found in an unrenewed mind; it is only a renewed mind that can discern and control the heart when it's going astray.

Romans 12:2[AMP] – And do not be conformed to this world [any longer with its superficial values and customs], but be transformed and progressively changed [as you mature spiritually] by the renewing of your mind [focusing on Godly values and ethical attitudes], so that you may prove [for yourselves] what the will of God is, that which is good and acceptable and perfect [in His plan and purpose for you].

It represents the word of God engrafted into you, the knowledge of His will established, and the strength of God in you. I stated in the preceding page the importance of knowing and walking in our divinely ordained purposes, and how it guarantees our victory over the enemy; the belt of righteousness plays an important role in that, hence, our purposes were predestined by God, and it therefore requires His word (i.e. alignment with His wisdom, and will for us and ways) to attain them. Renewing the mind must be seen as a core engagement because human minds are evil, corrupt, and dead. We cannot be free from its influence without consistently unlearning its ways and replacing them with God's patterns.

Proverbs 4:23b - it determines the course of our lives. GNT says – your life is shaped by your thoughts.

Meaning that, for our lives to be what God has designed them to be, we must submit to His word, allowing it to correct, teach, discipline, instruct and shape us thereby; making our decisions and choices on the strength of His omniscience.

If you don't withstand the battles of the mind, your life will toss about. Being a Christian didn't promise a life of no challenges and difficulties, these things are living with us in the world. The good news is that we can still overcome them as long as we take our stand on God's word, as a rock to keep us from being shaken. Read also, Ephesians 4:14[AMP], 2 Corinthians 10:5[AMP]

The Message translation of 2 Corinthians 10: 5 gave a very befitting interpretation, it says – The world is unprincipled. It's dog-eat-dog out there! The world doesn't fight fairly. But we don't live or fight our battles that way-never have and never will. The tools of our trade aren't for marketing or manipulation; they are demolishing that entire massively corrupt culture. We use our powerful God-tools to smash warped philosophies, tear down barriers erected against the truth of God, fitting every loose thought and emotion and impulse into the structure of life shaped by Christ. Our tools are ready at hand for clearing the ground of every obstruction and building lives of obedience into maturity.

Joseph had that tool, the belt of truth and breastplate of righteousness, self-control, and contentment, he used it to smash the contrary voice of immorality, and he fled from Potiphar's wife, no need to negotiate with sin, the offer was quite an interesting one, very attractive, but the word of God overflowing in him says no to that offer and as wise and obedient as he is- he agreed with the No. The Breastplate of righteousness is a symbol of purity (before God and man) Psalm 25:21[NLT] - says- May integrity and honesty protect me; for I put my hope on you.

Joseph refused to compromise his standard; he remained faithful to God during the trial and temptation seasons of his life. Those who sincerely depend on God live their lives reverently, with full confidence that there's more to what they are going through. God has prepared a special blessing for those who walk uprightly, something bigger than victory over devils- Matthew 5:7- Blessed are those who hunger and thirst for righteousness: for they shall be filled.

He promised to satisfy them with every good thing [PS103:5] Every righteous man has the eyes of God fixed on them and His hands working for them [1 Samuel 16:18, 2:26, Luke 2:40], righteous men (those in right standing with God in thoughts and deeds) are fearless because they know that the Lord is with them, that's why David was never afraid of the giant. It brings out the uniqueness in you, improves your character, makes you attractive so that people will love to be around you; robs off the beauty of God on you, and makes you easily favoured; men see your trustworthiness.

Psalm 41:12 says- As for me, you have upheld me in my integrity and set me in your presence forever. God upholds men of integrity and sets them before His presence, where no harm or devil can destroy them. Anyone who honours God, in turn, receives honour from men both great and small; He secures their lives and makes sure they dwell in His presence forever. Ecclesiastes 2:26a says- To the man who pleases Him, God gives wisdom, knowledge and happiness, but to the sinner He gives the task of gathering and storing up wealth to hand it over to the one who pleases God (NIV).

The world's principle says that for one to be wealthy, one must accumulate wealth; while Christ's principle says that you must be a giver, your life must be impactful, and you would have to sow bountifully to reap bountifully. They recognize wealthy men by their net worth, but God counts wealth by the number of people your life blesses, and transforms for the better and His glory, not for fame or any other ulterior motives. Christ's principle is foolishness to the world.

The traditions of men are some people's belt or shield; they build their lives on it and are so blinded by them that they don't see clearly, and this eventually brings hopelessness into their lives by the time it starts disappointing them because everything that comes from nature has an expiration date and is limited.

Many are entangled today by the deceit of the world and the cheap lies of the devil, especially when they seek validation and comfort from the world; they've been lured into so many illicit acts and habits and even addiction because they thought they could find solace or some level of satisfaction and approval in them.

The ideology of the world says that taking revenge when hurt is the best cure for bitterness, while God's way is that forgiveness is the best cure for bitterness and letting God avenge us.

The world contradicts the word because it can't understand it, it takes the Spirit of God for one to understand and believe the scriptures. Did you know that in Luke 24, it was real that the disciples of Christ never really believed in or understood clearly all He'd been foretelling while with them.

Despite the message delivered by the angels through Mary and others, despite their visit to the tomb (after receiving the message from the women) and all the evidence (proving that Christ has risen) they were still not sure of what happened-they were in absolute confusion and doubt.

Even when Jesus was standing with them they were still not confident. Verse 25 says that Jesus called them foolish-meaning "sluggish in mind, dull in perception" He also called them slow of heart to believe – meaning "slow of heart to adhere to and trust in and rely on". Truly, had it been they strongly believed or grasped what both the prophets and Christ Himself had predicted concerning His death and resurrection, they would have anticipated for that moment, and expected to see the miraculous power of God through the resurrection of Christ from the dead.

However, they lost hope when Christ died; in fact, they probably doubted the possibility of Christ's resurrection, maybe because there was no prophet in mind (at that point) that could raise Christ, or possibly because the trauma of Christ's terrible death on the cross they witnessed engulfed them. No matter the situation, it is the Holy Spirit that gives light to the human spirit to understand the things of the spirit.

The Holy Spirit is the power of God, and whenever the Word is spoken, the power of God flows into or works on it to make it bud and blossom. Bishop David Oyedepo states in one of his teachings that the word of God is the original source of power which is the factor for dominion; that the Holy Ghost empowers our access to what God has said.

In the beginning, the power of God manifested Himself in His word, the waters by which the Spirit of the Lord hovered were the word of God, in essence, the Holy Spirit broods over the word of God to help us access the ones that apply to our circumstances so that we can dominate them.

God has given us His word, and we should treasure it as our greatest life asset. If you know, believe in, rely on, and live God's word- you're automatically a powerful being. The devil is afraid of those who know how to use the word; the word of God when rightly applied is the secret of great success. King David understood this secret and he never failed to utilise the word of God, but earnestly desired to improve in its knowing, meditating and acting on it. Let the word of the Lord be written at the board of your hearts, let it serve as your guide. The belt of righteousness and the breastplate of righteousness in place are what guarantee our standing firm. Read Romans 3:10-18(NIV).

This is unrighteousness defined in this scripture; the scripture clarifies that all have sinned; both Jews and gentiles are in bondage. It explains and teaches that all people possess a sinful nature that draws them towards sin and evil; which results in guilt and condemnation. God's response to this tragic situation is to offer forgiveness, help, grace, and salvation to all through the redemption that is in Christ Jesus (Romans 3).

Now, why does the deplorable condition of humanity continue? Simply because there is no fear of God; if there is, men would seek reconciliation and peace. (PR 16:6; 3:7) Through the fear of the Lord, a man knows righteousness. Romans 3:21 says- But now righteousness from God, apart from the law, has been made known, to which the law and prophets testify.

The phrase "righteousness from God" refers to God's redemptive activity in the sphere of human sin by which He, in a just way, puts us in a right relationship with Himself and liberates us from the evil power, "where the working of salvation and the manifestation of righteousness are essentially the same thing.

This revelation of God's righteousness in the scriptures is not something that has ended; as the power of God for salvation that accompanies the believer, it is constantly fresh and relevant. We, however, receive or become righteous through faith in Christ Jesus; it is not a title anyone can give but can only be given by God Himself. God determines who is or is to become righteous.

As a matter of fact, righteousness in God is an act of faith, while faith in God births righteousness, where without these two- it is impossible to please God. Abraham's faith was absolutely radical; it endured, trusted, obeyed, fought, was fearless, hopeful, and was full of gratitude and glory to God. This type of faith receives the reward of God's power and ability working in favour for those who manifest it.

When a man lives to please God, God gives him victory without a fight (2 kings 19:35; Eccl 2:26). There are so many things that come with righteousness, it brings peace, comfort, progress, health, long life etc., it reveals God's wisdom on a man and distinguishes a man among others. As you put on the breastplate of righteousness (being watchful over what comes in and goes out of your heart) may the peace and joy in Christ flood your heart, Amen!

8

GOSPEL OF PEACE

With your feet fitted with the readiness that comes from the gospel of peace {Ephesians 6:15}. These guidelines in Ephesians 6 are secrets of good living, fulfilling purpose, and great victory in Christ the Lord. None should be dissented or is to be regarded as irrelevant, but must be accepted by all believers.

Believers are not people who simply attend church meetings on Sundays, but are representatives of Christ, having the express image and likeness of Christ, ambassadors of His heavenly kingdom here on earth, His elect, chosen ones, predestined by God, partakers of Christ's death, life, suffering, and glory, and co-heirs with Christ. Romans 8:28-30 (NIV)

Beloved, if you have been engrafted in Christ, (regenerated into God's family/kingdom) count yourself blessed to be on the winning team, Praise God! Having this in mind, putting on the whole armour points to your responsibilities according to God's expectations and provisions.

The shoe of readiness is one armour and weapon God gave believers to fight with as soldiers since we wrestle against forces of darkness for the salvation of souls, restoration of peace between man and God, 2 COR 5:18b – And God has given us this task of reconciling people to him. The readiness comes from the power the gospel supplies to our spirit. This gospel produces faith [Romans 10:17], i.e., spiritual stability, that was why Apostle Paul was determined to preach it.

It produces faith in both its speaker and the hearer because it is the power of God unto salvation. The ability to believe in God's love, in Christ, and in the victory He had wrought comes from hearing and preaching the gospel. 1 Corinthians 9:16- [NLT], 1 John 5:4-5[NLT], Romans 10:13-15[NLT]

The feet of these messengers are beautiful because it is fitted, well fastened to drive the course of God on earth, preparing themselves and others for the Lord. They dwell on the mount of God, receiving the oracle from God; they are heralds of glad tidings.

From Habakkuk 2:1-2[NLT], it is obvious that believers have no option when it comes to preaching the good news of Christ, the Spirit of truth compels us to do so, and the Holy

Spirit testifies about Christ therefore He does this through us, His subjects. I have met certain Christians arguing about the topic of preaching the gospel; the preacher on the pulpit was teaching that spreading of Gospel is compulsory for every believer while this set of people insisted that it isn't. Now few of their excuses were:

1. They are workers in the church especially, as singers, they are already passing the message across to people

2. While some said that everyone has a different calling, in the sense that not everyone is gifted to evangelise.

Now looking at what the scripture (as the foundation and doctrine for Christians) says concerning the spreading of the Gospel in Mark 16:15 – and He said to them, go into all the world and preach and publish openly the good news (the Gospel) to every creature (of the whole human race)

This means that being a church worker does not stop you from telling others about Christ, sharing the good news with others is proof that the Spirit of truth is in you and that you're a proud child of God, who is not ashamed to tell others of the marvellous things you benefit through Christ. Being a church worker, however, gives you more platforms to work for the establishing of souls (1 Peter 4:10).

Romans 8:28-30 says it all. *Those He foreknew, He predestined, those He predestined, He called, those He called, He justified, those He justified, He glorified.* If you were not called, how would you have answered? It is only those who are called are the ones who can answer; there is no other special calling to preach because Romans 10:8 says "The message is very close at hand; it is on your lips and in your heart".

When you receive salvation and are baptised in the Holy Ghost, remember John 16:14 says that the Holy Spirit, the Spirit of truth, will glorify Christ by receiving from what is Christ's and will give to you (paraphrased). This means that He shares with you the joy, peace, secrets, victories, and glories of Christ including His burden, suffering, sorrow, and desires; the burden of Christ becomes your burden so that when you yield your heart to Him, Christ will use you for His glory.

In John 4 the Samaritan woman whom Jesus met at the well, after hearing from Jesus, after Jesus had revealed Himself to her, this woman left her jar to testify to others the encounter she had had. Verse 39 says that numerous Samaritans from that town believed in and trusted in Him because of what the woman said when she declared and testified, "He told me everything that I ever did."

So stop giving excuses that you've not been called or that you're a worker in the church: go into the world and testify to the unbelievers and win souls for Christ. Every God's plan/purpose always points to His rescue strategies; the gifts

He gives are for the betterment of humanity. Read Matthew 5:14-16[NLT], Romans 12:4-8 (AMP)

He who exhorts (encourages), to his exhortation; he who contributes, let him do it in simplicity and liberality, he who gives aid and superintends, with zeal and singleness of mind; he who does acts of mercy, with genuine cheerfulness and joyful eagerness.

Therefore, every notion that suggests that we all have different purposes regarding whether to share the good news or not is a demonic thought that is mounted to distract the church from the vision God has given us through Christ.

Yes, we have different gifts, but we have one Spirit, one goal, one belief, and one doctrine, one value; and are meant to serve the purpose of kingdom growth, popularisation (depopulation of hell), and both spiritual and physical soundness of God's people. So therefore, the gift(s) God deposited in you amplifies your essence as a child of God.

Mathew 28:19-20 saying-19 Go then and make disciples of the nations, baptising them into the name of the Father, and of the Son, and of the Holy Spirit, teaching them to observe everything that I have commanded you, and behold, I am with you all the days {perpetually, uniformly and on every occasion}, to the very close and consummation of the age. Amen (so let it be).

In our respective homes, we work together to achieve common goals; we make diverse plans and strategize on how to carry them out because we are family, and when we do this, we enjoy the different abilities of everyone and each other's company. This unity and having one voice is rewarded with limitless progress.

Likewise, you are a diplomat of God here on earth, what determines how successful you'd be is the quality of your relationship with God and your submission to His patterns. Being an ambassador is a lot to handle, for instance- a company chooses a brand ambassador to be the "face" of the brand, who is capable of influencing its buying and selling. They have trusted sources of information and are highly rewarded. They use their initiatives, creativity, connections, and already-established networks to market the brand via word-of-mouth marketing tactics and through different media, representing the brand positively in a multitude of settings, performing product representation in certain events, etc. The more the brand he represents grows, the more recognition he will gain from the company. The company makes sure that they get paid according to the agreement, either by commission or salary.

Every follower of Christ is a face chosen by God to represent Christ and His kingdom, so, we engage our circles, networks, and media to positively demonstrate the fullness of Christ to the world, not just our circles alone. Therefore, you must be passionate about kingdom growth, and be willing to spend and be spent, as it may require some level of sacrifice from you. God desires peace with all men; it is your responsibility to tell them that. God has placed you in charge of the world, you can start somewhere like your family, neighbourhood, village, etc.

The Apostles waxed stronger and stronger in spreading the gospel despite all the obstacles and territorial oppositions, these people did not have all the means we have today, they didn't have the technology, yet they didn't settle for limitations. But today, we have an easier life like cars, aircraft including the internet and so on. Our glory and fulfilment lie in doing the will of God.

There are unlimited blessings to those who are fighting on the Lord's side in saving and restoring others. If the Apostles needed fire to do this, the church should pray for even more fire to be released because the end time is drawing near and the world's perversion has greatly increased, even the Church will not be safe if they do not buckle up.

The early church and our church today are nothing to be compared with: their time was the time people leave everything (and also used everything) they have to serve God. And believe me, the more their passion, and efforts; the more the power of God manifested in them. These people left a legacy and so must we: we must bring back the zeal, love, and purity of the early church to this era.

HOW DOES PREACHING THE WORD HELP YOU AS A BELIEVER?

1. It establishes the consciousness that you have peace with God through your relationship with Christ, by His death and resurrection – Ephesians 2:8-10.

2. It builds your knowledge and understanding, God Himself takes His time to teach you as you devote your time to learn. There are problems only what you know can solve, without praying and fasting- Isaiah 54:13, 2 Timothy 2 15.

3. It boosts your faith, as you speak to others, the Holy Spirit speaks to you, He let the word minister to you before it ministers to others- 1 John 5:4.

4. It creates an opportunity for you to always be in God's presence, whereby He supplies you with strength, revelation, and comfort. He takes care of all your spiritual, emotional and all round needs.

5. It gives you the boldness to communicate with God more as a kingdom partner, not every believer has that privilege, because partners have more recognition than the ordinary, and their prayers are answered because they're being taught by the Holy Spirit what the will of God is, and they pray it into reality. Partners don't bother too much about themselves; they are burdened with God's burden, so when they pray answers come immediately.

6. God is very jealous for them i.e. He guards them zealously because they are His assets, He fights for them by Himself because they made God their friend/ally- Psalm 91:14-16.

7. It fills your life with joy, many people don't know that joy is a weapon that can be used against the enemy, this is one thing I was taught in a revelation, that the more joyful I am, the higher I soar spiritually that the enemies cannot have access to or reach me and it helps you connect with the Holy Spirit and creates no room for the devil's wiles of worry and anxiety.

Jesus fills your life with joy and peace because you are His witness, as heaven rejoices – you too rejoice, many times I experience this joy in my life, sometimes I'd feel like shouting at the top of my voice, and songs flowing from my heart, sometimes I'd feel like dancing as I walk down the road from evangelism, this experience is priceless; it made me understand that the joy that Jesus gives is different from the joy we feel when material or physical blessings and promotions come our way, it is completely exceptional. (John 14:27, 15:11, Isiah 61:3, Luke 15:7, and Psalm 45:7)

Congratulations to those who are engaging themselves in doing this heartbeat of God; who see it as a privilege, and do it as the Master bids, this actually establishes certain levels of guarantee for you. The list of ways this readiness makes you victorious is endless; you have to make your discoveries as you practise what you're reading now.

To answer a child of God is not by words, many have sacrificed their all and themselves too for the sake of the gospel, and the gate of hell has never prevailed, Jesus is consistent in building His church by the power of God unto salvation, which is the Gospel. Nations, kings, and rulers of a different sort have come and gone with their laws and policies, but the church is still and will continue to march on till Jesus comes for her.

Nonetheless, you have the choice or opportunity to join Christ in His agenda for the world and against the kingdom of darkness. God will count you among His great ones, His faithful and wise servant. What baffles me a lot is how people call themselves children of God and yet are ashamed to tell others about Him: It is an error that needs immediate acknowledgment and correction. Friend, resolve in your heart to be a real asset in God's house rather than an equator, a mirage, because we are saved to help others get saved, not to argue about position in church.

If Christ had not died, no one would be saved; if the apostles had neglected their God-given assignments and just occupied seats/offices - many souls would have died without experiencing the love of the Father, so all hands must be on deck according to the grace we've received; it takes a decisive one to make a difference and God will align and honour your steps.

Preaching the word equips you, the enemy is afraid of those who know too much about God and of those who are manifestos of His power, wisdom, and love. Some Christians ignorantly despise their spiritual birth right like Esau. The reason God said "Esau I hate, Jacob I love" is not because He is partial, but because He foreknew that Esau would despise His divine purpose (his birth right) for things that counted not so much, he was reluctant and careless with his life and choices.

You know, people don't just inherit possessions from their fathers simply because they're a member of that family, I've seen company owners who wrote their wills to people who are not related to them because those people were responsible enough to prove to the owner that they could manage the company or property.

Therefore they gained the trust of the owner of the company while the sons, who are supposed to be an heir were busy doing nothing, and feeling entitled to everything, well, they were disappointed at last; they lost what was supposed to be their inheritance to a stranger because they didn't think it was necessary to prove to their father that they can sustain the company and continue with its vision. They assumed that everything would eventually be theirs; this is indeed a costly assumption that believers should avoid completely.

Many are ashamed of Christ; they hide their belief from friends and family; they prefer not to say they're Christians because they're afraid of being mocked or rejected, they hide their Bibles not because they'll be persecuted if they're caught but because of friends and to gain material things from them. God cannot be mocked, and He knows exactly those who are His; He is watching you and is weighing everything you are doing with the free will He gave you. Jesus said something remarkable in Mark 8:34-38(KJV).

The day I understood that angels rejoice over one soul that is saved, I began to picture in my mind how it would be up there. I imagined how they'd shout or sing to God, maybe throwing flowers and pleasant fragrance all over, or maybe blowing a happy trumpet to Jesus. I imagined that each time a soul is won, all the heavenly beings will begin to praise Jesus for all the price He paid for mankind, maybe flying around in more stylish forms.

So I said to myself, "I can throw a beautiful party in heaven just by preaching to others and winning them for Christ. With God's strength and wisdom backing me up, I knew that if I could make God happy, I too would always be happy no matter what. Preaching the gospel and winning souls for Christ is a way to reward Him for His soul, for His sacrifice.

Truthfully, eyes have not seen, ears have not heard, and minds have not conceived what God has prepared for those who love Him and prove it by going from street to street, road to road, one nation to another, etc., sharing the gospel of peace to the world, reconciling men to their maker (1 Corinthians 2:9).

Every soul that you win for Christ is a fruit unto salvation and Jesus has promised that He will prune you to continue to bear fruit in yourself and others all for His glory. Your success as a believer is not determined by the amount of wealth you have amassed; it is weighed by how much heaven feels your impact; it shows how relevant you are to God, and that is what will determine if you're displaceable or not. Being a fruit-bearing branch makes you sustainable, it preserves you.

9

THE SHIELD OF FAITH

In addition to all this, take up the shield of faith, with which you can extinguish all the flaming arrows of the evil one, (Ephesians 6: 16). I've read many books and have seen how different authors have tried to explain what faith is, and they're all inspiring and correct. One thing to note about faith is that it works with the level of what we know, and how much we know God.

Faith began with God from the beginning, and it's still sustained by God. Faith goes beyond trying your luck or guessing, but as Hebrews 11:1 says – it is being certain, being sure, Faith is the evidence, the force that quickens or brings to existence what you can see.

When you believe in Jesus – that faith activates and establishes you as a believer, a righteous- child of God. Matthew 8: 5 – 10 has a record of faith that amazed Jesus. One of those books I read defines faith as a currency to buy from heaven. Very true, this man's faith brought healing to his servant, the woman who was bleeding to death, and many other people.

I want to ascertain that faith is not just a currency but it is a lifestyle, a pattern of living that God sets for those who desire to follow Him. Faith goes beyond getting our needs or problems solved; it is the character of a believer that makes him a God-pleaser. Everything we have in Christ and how far we can go with Him begins with and still depends on our faith. Three important factors that generate faith in any man, whether believer or not, include:

1. Knowledge: through critical learning and studying someone's faith can sprout, e.g. you invite people to church, and after the teaching or sermon you see them responding to God maybe by adjusting their ways, answering altar calls, and stuff like that. It happened because they caught the light.

2. Understanding: the centurion is a good example here, he, by understanding (his practice), knew that Jesus has or operates under authority, and he knew by experience that Jesus has the power to heal, of course, he must have seen or heard the news of the miracles; he knew that every man in power always has people under them and is always obeyed, so he believed with all certainty that Jesus would also have people who are under him and will obey Him, that was why he didn't bother Him about coming, knowing that His words are enough to accomplish great wonders.

The more you practise what you know, the better understanding you'll gain. Knowing is not enough, because having an understanding of something speaks of your skilfulness or expertise, something you're very good at, doing something with less effort and more results – that is understanding. So after you study and learn, go beyond knowing and practise your knowing into understanding.

3. Love: What is faith? It is the ability to act according to God's will, you know His will or commands and you act on it. There were men in the scripture who knew God and the Bible recorded that they walked with God blamelessly, people like Enoch, Abraham etc. this is not ordinary faith only to get our needs and our miracles done, it is faith inspired by love – Romans 5:5.

If you search through the scripture, you'd see many who got different blessings by their faith in God, when those blessings came eventually they began to dishonour God and that was their end while some others gave up all that they had to follow and serve God. You see, nothing can truly separate such persons from God's love – Romans 8:38-39. Zachariah and Elizabeth served God blamelessly even though at their old age they still had no child, this is the faith that equips believers to overcome the wicked one.

Apostle Paul urged that every believer (who is also a soldier of Christ) should always carry the shield of faith. Every soldier always has a shield to stop the spears that the enemy throws at him. In the same way, you have to always trust God. Whenever you do that, it is like you are holding up a shield that stops the things that the devil throws at you. They are like burning spears, but if you trust God, he will stop them and put them out –Ephesians 6:16; PEV).

THE FIERY SPEARS OF THE EVIL ONE AND ITS EFFECTS

Knowing this will help you be more aware of the devil's attempt on you, and will help you walk victoriously consciously. As explained earlier, the aim of his darts is to kill, steal from and destroy every human, whether saved or not. That is why, for us humans to be on the safe side, we must agree in faith, in accordance with God's word, when we agree with God (that's faith), we disagree with the devil no matter his facts and proofs.

Some of the things he throws includes-; envy, gossip, greed, sickness and death, defeat, thoughts, despair, doubt, lies, lack of love, addiction, pride etc. they are too numerous to mention; but when you hold up your shield of faith- his plans and the effect of his arrows against you are put out.

THE SHIELD OF FAITH - WHY? The shield of faith represents your stability on God's word, your reliance on His promises, your trust in His plans, and your submission to his patterns and processes. Everything humans do begins with the mind; the decisions we make, our desires, our actions, and our responses to things all begin with the mind. When we comply with God to lead and help us- we are subjecting our will to Him, in that way, there would be no room for the evil one.

THINGS TO DO TO GROW YOUR FAITH

1. Study God's word and let it occupy your thoughts.

2. Seek and fellowship with the Holy Spirit; He put life in your faith; any faith without the Holy Spirit is lifeless. You will know Him in person and He will speak the truth to you, you will hold on to the truth against the lies the devil throws at you or tempts you to say.

3. Study yourself, learn your weakness and tackle it with divine counsels found in God's word.

4. Put your mind on heaven and or on heavenly things – Colossians 3:1, Hebrews 11:10.

5. Love God wholeheartedly and love men genuinely.

6. Prayer always strengthens you spiritually, your body may be weak, but if you're strong spiritually – it will flow to your other parts. Jesus overcame temptations not just because He is Jesus, but because He always prayed (Matthew 26:41).

Faith establishes God's nature and phenomenality in our hearts. The level of faith of each individual differs as it is determined by how much we know and acknowledge Christ. In the beginning, the earth was made by faith, God called forth things as they were in His imagination. For instance – during creation, God had pictured beauty, life, light, all the things He called into existence already existed in His mind. Those things were not there physically, He called them forth (e.g., let there be light) according to how He predestined them to be, and they came to pass. Romans 4:17c (KJV) and calleth those things which are not as though they were.

God also hopes in His words, He watches over His word in expectation, for it to accomplish what He sends it to do – Isaiah 55:10-11 says – For as the rain cometh down, and the snow from heaven, and returneth not thither, but watereth the earth, and maketh it bring forth and bud, that it may give seed to the sower and bread to the eater: so shall my word be that goeth forth out of my mouth; it shall not return unto me void, but it shall accomplish that which I please, and it shall prosper in the thing whereunto I sent it.

In the sense that, when He said let there be light, He looked to see if the light had come and if it was exactly as He expected; that is why the Bible said "and God saw the light and it was good."

I call Abraham's faith "stupid faith". Stupid means lacking intelligence. Abraham's faith in God was so strong that he did not have to figure anything out with humanistic knowledge or intelligence; he wasn't wise in his own eyes, and that is the kind of stupidity that pleases God, and He uses this type of stupidity to confound the wise and to shame the proud.

The devil thought that he knew God's plan and that killing Jesus would scatter God's plans. He blinded the eyes of the priest and the crowd, and they screamed, "Crucify Him!" Not knowing that God had already set up his (the devil's) downfall through that. Jesus laid down His life willingly, put His trust in the Father, and followed His plans. For us to be victorious, we must grow to the level of following God stupidly, that level when His will is all that matters, and you'll see how the devil will live in terror and defeat.

The belt of truth, the breastplate of righteousness, readiness for the gospel of peace, the helmet of salvation, and the sword of the Spirit- they are active and powerful once your faith is active; your faith is the control room, and it keeps you under control. Your thoughts, desires, actions, ambitions, emotions, everything is put under the control of God by your faith in Him.

Those who know their God shall be strong, and do exploits (Daniel 11:32b). Many children of God are not manifesting the power and blessings of God today the way they ought to because of faithlessness; in Matthew 17:17,20 Jesus called His disciples" faithless and perverse people, today they believe- tomorrow they're doubting and unbelieving. This shows how much unbelief displeases God; it is proof that they didn't completely trust God. Jesus pointed out that unbelief or doubt is a form of perversion/corruption.

Devil corrupts the mind of men and shifts their trust in God and replaces it with fear, anxiety, doubt, etc. Now, instead of them acting in faith, they leave their hearts open to demonic manipulations. However, I was encouraged to know that there's a solution to this deprival, in verses 19-20, after Jesus had freed the demon-possessed man that was brought to Him, His disciples approached Him privately out of curiosity to understand why they couldn't cast out that demon, and Jesus said "you don't have enough faith (unbelief), if you had faith even as small as a mustard seed, you could say to this mountain, 'move from here to there', and it would move. Nothing would be impossible.

Of course, you know how very little mustard seed is, this means that they had no faith at all, probably they were doing try-your-luck games, because if it's not faith, it is not faith – very lifeless, dead works. God tests the faith of His people; He tested the faith of King Saul (1 Samuel 13), Jesus tested the faith of His followers (Mark 4:35-40), and even the faith of the entire Israelites was tested (Numbers 13); our faith is rewarded when it stands above what we hear, see, or feel, like that of Caleb and Joshua.

Peradventure, you have failed in many ways because of fear, unbelief, pressure, and the like. All you have to do is seek the solution in God's word, as the disciples did. The book of Acts is proof that they grew beyond their fears and limitations and conquered the evil one with the shield of faith. We too can be like them; the Church today can achieve so much for God with its shield in place always.

So faith comes from hearing, that is, hearing the good News about Christ – Romans 10:17 [NLT]. If there's a hearing, that means there's seeking, listening, fellowship/communion, and closeness with the source of faith.

OTHER SOURCES OF FAITH

ENCOUNTER WITH GOD: (Jeremiah 1:9-12) Jeremiah was in his early 20s when God called him; he wasn't an influential personality in society and was only from an average home, his father Hilkiah was a priest; and they lived in the region of Anathoth in the tribe of Benjamin; So Jeremiah was an average boy whom God chose to show Himself to.

The text we read will make you think that God was speaking to one mighty, influential king or army, but you see, that is exactly how an encounter with God can change a man, from being timid and afraid to being bold and powerful. When God meets with a man, He comes with His fullness, in such a way that you'll be impacted by His visit. He comes with His glory and praise (He would introduce himself to you) (Isaiah 6:1-9), power, words of assurance and transformation, energy, and touch.

From that day, Jeremiah's perspective changed; his ambitions changed; Moses had a similar experience – God showed up when he thought how miserable his life had become, all that changed, the misery and feeling of defeat were dealt with at once; he got a new purpose, a second chance to make a difference and fulfil divine purposes.

God did not give Jeremiah machine guns, or bulldozers, nor was he a politician or an influential personality and stuff like that; – He gave him the assurance of His presence and His word [Jeremiah 1:7-8,12]. Through the authority in God's word, you can create, build, heal, raise, prosper, demolish, uproot, tear down, etc. Make time to study the word of God, not as a storybook, and be drowned in His presence as your life depends on it, the intimate knowledge of Christ is the revelation of God's glory and is meant to be your experience and testimony.

FASTING AND PRAYER: Whenever you see yourself struggling spiritually, it is a sign that there's been an attack on your faith. Isaiah 40:31 says- But those who wait for the Lord {who expect, look for, and hope in Him} shall change and renew their strength and power; they shall lift their wings and mount up {close to God} as eagles {mount up to the sun}; they shall run and not be weary, they shall walk and not faint or become tired {AMP}.

Fasting and prayer are other ways you can keep your mind, spirit, and body connected to heaven; you separate yourself from distractions and cut off from excesses that could hinder or limit your flow in the Holy Spirit. Either you fast and pray or you practise quiet time, it opens your heart as you wait on God.

Those who wait upon God are promised:

1. Strength to revive them amid exhaustion and weakness, and or of suffering and trial –Psalm 84:7, 2 Corinthians 12:8-10.

2. Great understanding and revelation- Habakkuk 2:1

3. The grace for sustainability - 2 Corinthians 12:8-10.

4. Also read Psalm 37:34, Isaiah 30:18, and Lamentation 3:25-26.

Understanding that a life of faith is not optional for believers; for the Bible says that the just shall live by faith {ROM 1:17; Habakkuk 2:4}.

If a man claims to be a child of God but without faith, such a person is not living a lie [2 TIM 3:5]. James 2:14-26 treats the ever-present problem of those among believers who profess to have saving faith in the Lord Jesus, yet manifest His power. Saving faith means a living, active, evident, and practical belief; it does not stop at confessing Christ as the saviour but also prompts obedience to Him as Lord.

Thus, obedience is an essential aspect of faith. Only those who trust can obey, and only those who obey can be trusted by God – John 4:23-24, Genesis 18:19. There is no contradiction between Paul and James regarding the topic of saving faith.

Apostle Paul emphasised faith as a means by which we accept Christ as saviour while James calls our attention to the fact that true faith must be an active and enduring faith that shapes our very existence in our walk with God and as pilgrims. Therefore, true saving faith cannot help but express itself in Godly action and devotion to Christ.

A deed without faith is a dead deed: faith without deeds is dead faith. James directed this teaching to redirect those in the church who professed faith in Christ and His blood atonement and believed that such a profession was all that was necessary for salvation. They believe that a personal, obedient relationship with Christ as Lord is not essential. The scripture says that such faith is dead and will produce neither salvation nor anything good. The only kind of faith that saves is "faith expressing itself through love for God and humanity" (Galatians 5:6).

However, we must not think that we maintain a living faith solely through our effort. The grace of God, the indwelling Spirit, and the intercession of Christ work in our lives to enable us to respond to God by faith from first to last {Romans 1:17} If we ever stop being receptive to God's grace and the Holy Spirit's leading, then our faith will die.

Abraham's righteousness came not from observing the law, but through faith and action working together in love. His willingness to sacrifice Isaac was an expression of his faith in and commitment to God. The book of James chapter 2 establishes that faith and action didn't save us; i.e., they were separate from each other; it contends instead for faith at work. Faith and deeds cannot be separated; the latter flow naturally from the former (Galatians 5:6).

These works refer to the obligations to God and to humans that are commanded in the scriptures and that proceed from a sincere faith, a pure heart, the grace of God, and the desire to please God. For Paul, works refer to a desire to gain favour and salvation through obeying the law by one's effort (as some think rather) than true repentance and faith in Christ; he taught that salvation does not rest solely on the merit of one's efforts but on God's grace.

Both Paul and James state emphatically that true salvation faith will inevitably produce righteous deeds. Faith in Jesus Christ as Lord and Saviour, accompanied by deeds by the grace of God and indwelling Spirit, guarantees our continuous victory, success, and intimacy with God.

A walk of faith is a walk in love, trust, courage, and a sound mind that quenches the fiery darts of the enemy. Every believer must always put on this shield always - to stand tall at last; and every human on earth can only be saved by his/her faith in the grace God has provided to humanity through Christ Jesus.

The shield of faith is also like the rod of Moses, the rod was all he had, however, it was just a rod, but the authority he received and his ability to use it made the rod alive. Your faith in the power and authority of God upon you is all you need to divide every red sea and be the hero you're chosen to be.

10

HELMET OF SALVATION

Take The Helmet Of Salvation And The Sword Of The Spirit, Which Is The Word Of God (Ephesians 6:17). The brain is intelligent and one of the most important, largest, and central organs of the human nervous system. It is the control room that helps us to remember, understand, choose, etc. while the mind is the centre of thoughts, feelings, perception, memories, awareness, judgement, intentions, and opinions, etc. the brain coordinates movements, feelings, and different functions of the body; while the mind refers to a person's conscience, and thought process.

The brain and the mind (heart or soul, as it is differently called) are compatible, the mind and the brain work simultaneously, and the brain releases to the mind while the mind also releases to the brain. These two components are like partners, but the difference is that the brain is visible while the mind is mental.

Now, this brings us to why the helmet is important for head protection, especially when we are in an environment or doing things that could be risky or endanger our safety. We use a man-made helmet to cover the head because it is physical, while we use a spiritual helmet for the mind. A helmet is a protective covering specifically worn on the head to protect the head from injury and also the brain, and ultimately the whole body will be preserved to some extent. God uses the things we can relate to to communicate spiritual things to our understanding.

Talking about the mind, as said earlier, it is unseen but could be revealed through one's actions, lifestyles, responses, etc. Romans 12:2(KJV)- And do not be conformed to this world:

but be ye transformed by the renewing of the mind, that ye may prove what is that good and acceptable and perfect, will of God.

The mind was not regenerated at conversion, but the spirit was born again; what the mind needed was to be transformed by its renewal. This process makes you anew, changes your ideology about life and existence, and gradually heals your mind from its corruption. More so, it strengthens in you the consciousness or awareness of who you have become in Christ and who you are modelled after, this is what rests as a crown, it is your pride and confidence – the things you know Christ has done for and given you.

PEV translation of Ephesians 6:17 interprets, 'And a soldier wears an iron hat that stops the enemy from hurting his head. Well, you remember that God has saved you. That will be like an iron hat for you, to keep you safe.' This is important for us to note because this is one of the ways we can resist the evil one and defeat him in his operations against our souls.

JN 10:10 reveals that there's something the enemy comes to steal from believers, but if you study Jesus' response to that He said

"I have come to give you life and more abundantly", Jesus didn't want us to lose focus on what we have, by not losing focus – the devil cannot steal from us. Who you are in Christ is your pride, and your confidence, and the devil cannot stand that when you constantly confess that to yourself.

The motive behind all devil's accusations is to make you feel worthless, to portray that old picture playing in your mind, now, instead of you moving forward- you'd be stuck in your past, then he would ignite the fire of doubt, fear, guilt, and all sorts of mental breakdown; but Jesus said, "No matter what the devil is doing, remember that I have given you my life in an overflowing measure; you don't have to agree with the devil anymore, like Apostle Paul, all you have to do is look forward and forget the things that are behind.

Revelation 12:10(NLT) Then I heard a loud voice shouting across the heavens, "It has come at last- salvation, power, the kingdom of our God, and the authority of his Christ. The accuser of our brothers and sisters has been thrown down to earth- the one who accuses them before our God day and night.

You must remember that your salvation has come, Satan has lost his power over your life, and the kingdom of God has come in you. You should begin to manifest the authority of Christ, which He has given you as His follower.

Don't let him tell you otherwise, whether you are poor or rich, sick or healthy, for as long as you believe in Christ – you are saved and you have His life in you; only this mind-set is enough to get you the great miracles that you seek.

Jesus said to the people who believed him, "You are truly my disciples if you remain faithful to my teachings.

And you will know the truth and the truth, and the truth will set you free."- JN 8:31-32[NLT). Holding unto the truth, the written word of God is your helmet of salvation, it protects your mind from lies, deceit, temptations, and demonic manipulations; it supports your faith, guides your emotions, and desires, and organises your life to be according to God's design.

ACTIVATING YOUR MENTAL SPIRITUAL HELMET – HOW?

• First off, you must be born again, born of water and the Spirit through your surrender to Jesus as your Lord and Saviour and your loyal commitment to Him by the Holy Spirit – Acts 2:38. And complete reliance on God's mercy and grace. The helmet was specially designed for only whoever will call on Jesus with a sincere heart.

• Live a life of thanksgiving, you don't show gratitude to God only when a need is met, choose a lifestyle of praise and appreciation to God because your name is written in heaven.

• When you are thankful, it builds you up to see the good (God's plan) in every situation; your thoughts become right, pure, true and excellent, etc. it is important to develop a habit of thinking quality thoughts about yourself, about others, about God and His kingdom.

• Then, confess the things Christ has taught you by His Spirit over your life. You need the word to keep the enemy in his lane, so you must confess, declare His word over yourself and also testify about Christ to others – the more you do- the more He'll teach you more things, and the more you know, the more powerful you'd become.

Putting on the helmet of salvation is one way we contend for our faith. 2 Corinthians 10:4-5 says (NKJV) – *for the weapons of our warfare are not carnal, but mighty through God to the pulling down of strongholds. Casting down imaginations and every high thing that exalteth itself against the knowledge of God bringing into captivity every thought to the obedience of Christ.*

We must be conscious of what goes and comes to our mind, in that way, we can cast down those thoughts which are not inspired by God.

In 1 Samuel 17, an unforgettable event that took place in Judah was recorded. The day the Israelites faced one of their worst nightmares, it was fearsome, they were in a helpless and almost hopeless situation, and all they needed was an intervention.

I had to think of the condition the Israelites were in at that moment- that moment when Goliath almost stole their pride, all their boasts, and all their testimonies with his ranting.

However, amid all this helplessness, anxiety, and silence, God proved His faithfulness; He restored their hope, rendered help to them, and took away their shame through a young man named David who understood the mystery of using the helmet of salvation.

David's whole trust and boast were in God, he trusted in divine armour and weapon; he didn't give in to the intimidations of Goliath, by those muscles, his size, and his threat, but he stood courageously before him. He declared unwaveringly how he would defeat Goliath, he also encouraged himself with the memory of how God has strengthened him as a shepherd boy to kill a bear and a lion that attempted on his sheep, so with that in mind, he knew that Goliath wouldn't be a big deal too.

All David's boast was on God and he saw it as an embarrassment that a mere mortal like Goliath will keep God's people in fright. Revelation 12:11 – And they have overcome (conquered) him by means of the blood of the Lamb and by the utterance of their testimony, for they did not love and cling to life even when faced with death (holding their lives cheap till they had to for their witnessing). When I read this account of David, I said indeed, it is a powerful and glorious thing to be a child of God; it pays, and there are lots of things to learn from David.

✓ Learn how to confess God's word over your life.

- ✓ Learn how to declare God's standards over circumstances.
- ✓ Learn how to share God's goodness with others.
- ✓ Learn how to channel your mind to your source- always connect with God.
- ✓ Learn how to grow with God – David grew into a mighty man of valour.
- ✓ Learn how to care for others and be concerned about them; David risked his life by taking up that challenge with Goliath.
- ✓ Learn how to serve others; he served his father and his elder brother. (Those who serve others are eventually the greatest).
- ✓ Learn how not to be moved by what you hear or see; have faith in God.
- ✓ Learn how to unapologetically declare God's will over your future/destiny.
- ✓ Learn how not to let other people's fear and opinion limit you and your experience with God.
- ✓ Learn how to be at peace with God, when you do – you can believe and can ask anything from Him.

THE SWORD OF THE SPIRIT: The scripture in verse 17 states that the sword of the Spirit is the word of God. The Holy Spirit has a major role to play for the word of God to be effective in the world and the hearts of men for us. Without Him, we would just read the scriptures like a storybook without transformation, impact, and encounter, without manifestation of His power in the world.

Jesus promised to send His Spirit to dwell among men and to bring the fulfilment of God's promises to the world and believers. Everything the Holy Spirit does is in tune with God's will, which can also be seen in the Holy Scriptures. The Sword of the Spirit Explained:

I. First of all, it is a spiritual weapon God has given to His soldiers (to believers) through which His will and rules are asserted on earth.

II. It is two-edged, i.e. it is both defensive and offensive.

III. It can pierce through anything and cannot be limited.

IV. It can justify and condemn- John 12:48-50.

V. It has the power to separate good from evil.

VI. It brings repentance and transformation – 2 Corinthians 11:23-26.

VII. It is the power of God manifest in His word – 1 Corinthians 2:1-5.

Hebrews 4:12(NLT) For the word of God is alive and powerful. It is sharper than the sharpest two-edged sword, cutting between soul and spirit, between joint and marrow. It exposes our innermost thoughts and desires. 2 Timothy

3:16-17(NLT) 16 All Scriptures is inspired by God and is useful to teach us what is true and to make us realize what is wrong in our lives. It corrects us when we are wrong and teaches us to do what is right. God uses it to prepare and equip his people to do every good work.

From the above scriptures, you can learn some of the purposes of the sword of the Spirit: i.e. to make believers strong and able to withstand the onslaught of Satan; to save souls, and give them spiritual strength to be mature soldiers for the Lord; and to fight corruption and evil in the world, and so on.

However, for these to be achieved, all Christian soldiers need rigid training to know how to properly handle the sword of the Spirit, "rightly dividing the word of truth"- (2 Timothy 2:15). Only then will it be an effective defence against evil and an offensive weapon to demolish strongholds of errors and falsehood – 2 Corinthians 10:4-5.

The idea behind the piercing and the penetrating is that it reaches the heart, the very centre of the action, and lays open the motives and feelings of those it touches. I have written this book and in my other books so much about the word of God, the whole thing is that there would be no Church without God's word; there would be neither life nor creation without it. Therefore, everyone needs it to live and keep living, especially the Church.

Some of the ways the Holy Spirit communicates with or the word to be more real to us is through his provision of:

Comfort- The Holy Spirit provides assurance and encouraging words in tune with the scripture in times when we're down-casted or discouraged, He enables us to put our emotions in balance. Because the Holy Spirit feels what we feel, He is empathetic and compassionate He knows exactly the perfect thing to say or do to give us reassurance and peace.

The Holy Spirit has an attribute of a mother, Isaiah 66:13, says- As one, whom his mother comforts, so will I comfort you; you shall be comforted in Jerusalem. Mothers love their children with a unique tenderness of heart; I remember days when my mom wouldn't go anywhere without me; she never wanted to lose sight of me, and her concerns when things seem to go wrong are also deeply felt, so that you would be concerned for her too.

She disciplined and corrected our disobedience or errors, provided for our needs even if it meant giving her all, worked hard to take care of me and my other five siblings after the demise of our father, and prayed earnestly for our success, with a lot of warfare prayers to secure our destinies in God's hands.

Most of the time, I don't make decisions without involving her, I always want to know her opinion, and she always confided in me, we spent memorable time together as friends, all my friends knew her because I made sure I introduced them to her, she easily forgives me all the days I offended her; she believed and trusted in me despite all our disagreement, she was my teacher and I was always inspired by her, her lifestyle, relationship with God, etc.

I can keep going on and on, but the point I want to share from my experience while growing up with my mother is that when I lost her, the Holy Spirit became all that to me; He said to me "Now I will be your mother." At that time, I had not grown so much in fellowshipping with the Holy Spirit, but as He continued to help me, I grew to know Him and love Him, and I can tell you - He is far better than any mother.

The character of mothers is very similar to His attribute; He is our standby, advocate, helper, teacher, counsellor, intercessor, strengthening, etc. He can also be likened to a shepherd; in Psalm 23 David used that metaphor to describe how much the Holy Spirit meant to him or represents in his life and that of believers.

John 16:7-11 (NIV) - 7 But I tell you the truth: It is for your good I am going away. Unless I go away, the counsellor would not come to you; but if I go, I will send Him to you. When He comes, He would convict the world of guilt in regard to sin and righteousness and judgement: In regard to sin, because men do not believe in me, in regard to righteousness, because I am going to the Father, where you can see me no longer and in regards to judgement, because the prince of this world now stands condemned.

The concept of why the word of God is referred to as the sword of the Spirit is based on the ministry of the Holy Spirit in using the word to achieve divine purpose on earth, over all creation, physical and spiritual. Using that word which can cut through the soul and spirit, He convicts the world of:

a) Sin: The Holy Spirit will expose sin and unbelief in order to awaken a consciousness of guilt and the need for forgiveness. A Conviction also makes clear the fearful results if the guilty persist in their wrongdoing. After conviction, a choice must be made. This will often lead to true repentance and a turning to Jesus as Lord and Saviour.

b) Righteousness: The Spirit convinces people that Jesus is the righteous son of God, resurrected, vindicated, and now the Lord of all. He makes them aware of God's righteousness in Christ, shows them what sin is and gives them the power to overcome the world, living in God's righteousness.

c) Judgement: The Spirit convinces people of Satan's defeat at the cross, God's present judgement of the world, and future judgement of the entire human race. The ministry of the Holy Spirit is encircled by God's word; Little wonder, the Bible says that He (The Spirit) will not speak on His own, but will speak whatever the Father has said and will also remind us always what Jesus has taught us.

2 Timothy 3:16-17 says- All scriptures are God–breathed and are useful for teaching, rebuking, correcting and training in righteousness, so that the man of God may be thoroughly equipped for every good word.

The inspired word of God is the expression of God's wisdom and character and is able to give wisdom and spiritual life through faith in Christ. It is also the infallible witness to His saving activity for humanity. No human words or declarations of religious institutions are equal to its authority. God's word must be received, believed, and obeyed as the final authority to all things pertaining to life and Godliness.

One cannot submit to Christ's Lordship without submitting to God and His word as the ultimate authority. The Holy Spirit being the inspirer of the word opens the mind to understand its mysteries. We must use the inspired word to conquer sin, Satan, and the world (James 1:21). At times, people say that God does not speak to them, well, that means you don't study the scripture. Hearing His voice audibly is the same as when you read and meditate on His word because it is still the Holy Spirit that interprets it for your digestion.

The phrase "the word of God", "word of the Lord", the word", refers to a variety of situations in the Bible. It refers first of all to everything God has said directly. When God spoke to Adam & Eve, that was the word of God; similarly, He spoke to Abraham, Isaac and Jacob, Moses, Israelites, etc. God also spoke through the prophets; when they addressed God's people, they usually prefaced their statement with "this is what the Lord says" or "the word of the Lord came to me". Likewise, the Apostles, even though they don't preface their words with "thus saith the Lord".

Paul's sermon to the people of Pisidian Antioch {Acts 13:16-41} created such a stir that the next Sabbath almost the whole city gathered to hear "the word of the Lord.". Paul also said to the Thessalonians that when you receive the word of God, which ye heard from us, you accept it not as the word of men, but as it is, "the word of God" {1 Thessalonians 2:13; Acts 8:25}.

Furthermore, everything Jesus spoke was the word of God, for He is, after all, God. Jesus, unlike the prophets, introduced His saying with "I tell you"; in other words, He had divine authority within Himself to speak the word of God.

Indeed, Jesus is so closely identified with the word of God that He is called "the word" (JN 1:1). The Bible from beginning to end is the word of God, whether a writer used the phrase Moses said David said, or the Holy Spirit said made no difference. When an anointed minister is preaching or teaching- he is saying God's word. This book you're reading now automatically is God's word because it is God's breath.

The test to determine if God's truth is proclaimed in any sermon is whether it corresponds with the Holy Bible. The word of God stands firm in the heavens (Ps 119:89) yet, it is not static; it is dynamic and powerful and accomplished great things {Isaiah 55:10-11}.

The word of God creates and sustains what is created, it gives or imparts new life, and it releases grace, power, and revelation by which believers grow in their faith and commitment to Jesus Christ; in other words, it is a food that nourishes the soul, spirit, and body; lives and destinies depend on it to survive and thrive even in the midst of opposition and impossibilities.

It is the believers' sword given to us by which we contend against Satan and our old selves to stand for Christ; by this same word God will judge those who reject Him {John 12:48}, it judges the thoughts and intents of the man {Hebrews 4: 12}, in other words, those who choose to ignore God's ways will one day experience it as the word of condemnation.

The Bible described in an unmistakable language how we should react or respond to the scripture, {God's word} in all its different forms.

i. We must eagerly hear the word of God {Acts 17:11-12; Jeremiah 7:1-2; Habakkuk 2:1}.

ii. Seek to understand it {Matthew 13:23}.

iii. Praise it {Psalm 56:4, 10}.

iv. Love it; delight in it {Psalm 119:16, 47}.

v. Accept and treasure it.

vi. Trust in it and put our hope in its promises.

vii. Above all, we must obey what it commands and live according to it.

God calls those who minister the word to handle it correctly and to preach it faithfully; all believers are called to proclaim God's word wherever they go {Acts 8:4]. According to Isaiah 55:10-11; God does not sow vain seeds, His words are seeds that can never be unfruitful but yield His desire, purpose, or will upon all things. Truth is, there is so much to know about God's word.

11

PRAYING IN THE SPIRIT

Pray in the spirit on all occasions with all kinds of prayers and requests; be alert and keep praying for the saints (Ephesians 18). People have different notions about prayer, because of their upbringing, environment, and religious beliefs and practices. I'm convinced that for us to truly get the best result on prayer from- understanding it and its dynamics is key.

Prayer is a need. In my walk with God; I've truly understood that prayer is a need. It is a need we express to no one else but God. We have needs that only the touch of God can heal. When we are lonely, we need friendship, we have needs for our families, friends, society, and the world at large, and we have needs in our personal lives and relationship with God - God opened that door so that we could approach Him with all our frailty and longings.

Before the early church began, the teachers of the law and the Pharisees made their gatherings a place of judgement, to remind men of the consequences of their wrong actions and to judge the guilty ones. Their prayers are mostly routine recitations; there was never a need attached to them. It wasn't a need for them but just a practice— something they

139

would have to add to the program of the day; it carried no warmth, but just mere carnal words. It never changed them or anyone else. The Romans who lived among them never felt the impact of their gatherings as the Apostles fellowships were felt in Acts 2; they never impacted much of their people, nor were their gatherings attractive as they were full of discrimination. Jesus taught His disciples the essence of prayer, that prayer comes with a need, it must be seen as a need, and only then will it be heartfelt. He said 'These people honour me with their lips, but their hearts are far from me. Their worship is a farce, for they teach man-made ideas as commands from God (Matthew 15:8-9).

Without a doubt, we still have bible scholars and theologians who are like the Pharisees; they memorise the scripture, they're taught how to pray and preach, and do all sorts of religious rituals, but they lack the Pentecost experience. The Spirit is what differentiates between the Pharisees and the Apostles, between a bible scholar and an anointed Bible student – the Spirit makes the difference. Apostle Paul taught them saying "Pray in the Spirit on all occasions with all kinds of prayer and request...

He needed them to understand that there is no life in anything in which the Spirit is not involved, even as simple as praying may seem, it becomes dead, without life and lacking the right motive.

Praying in the Spirit:

• This implies praying with divine understanding; praying in the light of God. Remember, one of the Spirit's responsibilities is to guide, teach and reveal divine plans and patterns to the children of God. He makes us see our needs and depend on God for help and solution. Philippians 2:13- For it is God who works in you to do and to act in order to fulfil his good purpose [NIV].

• The Spirit won't stop at giving you understanding, but will give you the grace to believe in the possibility of what you're praying for; each time I pray, scriptures will flash through my mind, giving me a guarantee.

• He gives you the strength, right from within your bowels to pray fervently; it is the Spirit that quickeneth...

• He spreads the boldness that comes from Christ's love and mercy in our hearts so that we may come without guilt or shame.

Criteria for an effective prayer life include:

The Anointing: because this is a spiritual affair and can only be acceptable or productive when done in the Spirit, you need to be endued with power from on high −Luke 24:49, which means that the Holy Spirit will come upon you and fill you up.

The Spirit helps us in our weakness. We do not know what we ought to pray for, but the Spirit himself intercedes for us through wordless groans. And he who searches our hearts knows the mind of the Spirit, because the Spirit intercedes for God's people in accordance with the will of God- ROM 8:26-27(NIV). Jude 20 – But you, dear friends, by building yourselves up in your most holy faith and praying in the Holy Spirit.

The prayer made by the power of the Holy Ghost can never go wrong, because what you speak is the mystery of God, which cannot be grasped by the natural man. It exerts the will of God over His people and beyond, also, it edifies you- you open up your heart, and mouth for the Spirit to access you; it causes you to grow in faith, in your communion with God, the more you pray in the Spirit, the more familiar and close you'll be with Him.

When you pray in the Spirit, the Holy Spirit brings to your consciousness the desires of God, not just for you but concerning others, to intercede for others, praying according to the God-given desires of your heart, you would pray with divine love, which eliminates the possibility of selfishness in our prayers. And He sustains you with patient hope.

Knowing God's Word: for where a man's treasure is, there his heart will be. And out of the abundance of the heart – the mouth speaks. When you love His word, you will certainly know it and keep it in your heart; it will flow freely out of you.

Love and Mercy: As you receive from God, so you are expected to give the same, if not, you have put a hold on your side towards God (Read Matthew 9:13,12:7, Hosea 6:6, ISA 58)

Humility and Passion: He gives grace (i.e., show favour, preference) to the humble, and the passionate prayer of a righteous man He rewards greatly.

Partnership: This implies partnering with the Holy Spirit for the continuity and sustainability of what Jesus began and left off - one reward for this includes answers to prayers. Read - John 14:12- 14, 15:7-8.

Tongues Of Fire: Acts 1:8 "And you shall receive power when the Holy Spirit comes on you, and you will be my witnesses in Jerusalem, and in all Judea and Samaria, and to the ends of the earth." This promise came to pass in chapter two, tongues of fire rested upon each of them; they were filled with the Holy Spirit, Why? Jesus explained in chapter one, "You will be my witnesses, all over the earth.

Testifying for Christ means testifying against the evil one, Jesus had to empower His followers to be able to do this job, i.e., to establish the kingdom of God by contending against the devil over the souls and lives of men, to cast out devils, and so on. You need authority from God to do these things and that is why Jesus baptises His followers with fire. When the devil sees your fire, your strength and authority, he trembles because anything you say in Jesus' name – he must obey.

Remember, the name of Jesus does not work in the mouth of everyone, but only those who have been given the authority and fire. The Christian warfare against satanic forces calls for intensity in prayer. When you pray often, it helps your spirit be in tune with God, and it delivers you from spiritual coldness/Luke warmness, keeping your fire burning.

Why must I pray in tongues?

Judges 16:20(NLT) Then she cried out, "Sampson! The Philistines have come to capture you!" When he woke up, he thought, "I will do as before and shake myself free." But he didn't realise the Lord had left him. First off, praying in tongues is evidence that one is baptised (filled) in the Holy Spirit.

The anointing you have received from him remains in you..." (1John 2:27). We see here that Sampson, despite his long Nazarene hair, which is a symbol of God's power in his life, still had to shake himself to trigger the anointing. As for you, spirit-filled- the anointing is in your spirit, but it wouldn't work just by being there, that was why Apostle Paul in 2 Tim

1:6 reminded his son in the Lord, -Timothy to stir up the anointing in him continually.

One proven way to stir up the anointing is by speaking in other tongues; when you do, anything is possible, as the Bible says that those who are born of the Spirit are like the wind, very unpredictable. Bring out the extraordinary life you have, and don't settle for less – you are meant for signs and wonders.

HOW TO BE FILLED WITH THE HOLY SPIRIT

The truth you must know about this is that there's no mechanism to this, it's very simple and straight to the point. Luke 11:13- If you sinful people know how to give good gifts unto your children, how much more shall your heavenly Father give the Holy Spirit to those who ask him?

So the only way is to ask Him, you must know why you need Him, and your intentions must be genuine too. Then, for you to ask, you must first see the need, thirst for Him; when you're hungry, you find your way to the kitchen in search of or in preparation of the meal, you don't bother yourself with that when you're already full, you know and can tell the difference between staying hungry and being satisfied.

It is those who are thirsty and hungry who shall be filled; those who seek Him diligently are assured that they'll find Him. Therefore, that is the only way you can be baptised in the Spirit. JESUS IS THE BAPTIZER: Unfortunately, many have been deceived into believing that it is their pastor who baptises them. Your pastor is not the baptizer, only Jesus is; your Spirit-filled Pastor received his from the same source and can only be a channel by which God can open your heart to seeking Him so that the anointing is transferred to you. No matter how anointed a man is, if he lays His hand on you and your heart is not in tune or open to receive the baptism of the Holy Spirit – you'd end up wasting your time. Prior to the day I was baptised in the Holy Spirit, I had learned the importance of this infilling. As I studied on that subject, I became hungry; hungry to the extent that I would be all alone in the house, I would weep, my heart was broken and desperate, I would fast, pray, cry, and plead with God.

I would reject the food, even my very best food, then. But the day it finally happened, I had a witness within me that it would be that day. It was a church vigil, and I was filled with joy and excitement in advance – you feel when you see light shine over a situation, I had the conviction that I'd receive that special gift, I made sure that nothing took me away from that vigil. There and then, the atmosphere changed, and many others were taken over by the Holy Spirit, gifts were imparted. Tongues were loud in the room.

All of a sudden, the power of the Highest came upon me, I saw that I wasn't the one controlling what I was saying- I got the promise, what a glory! He promised that He will be our Emmanuel "He lives with you and will be in you" {John

14:17}. Jesus still fulfils this promise- only keep your heart ready.

TWO DIFFERENCES

John 20:22 refers to regeneration, which can be inferred from the phrase, "he breathed on them". The Greek word for "breathed" {emphusaō} is the same verb used in the Septuagint at Gen 2:7, where God breathed into Adam's nostrils the breath of life, and man became a living being. It is the same verb found in Ezekiel 37:9, where the slain was breathed into and they come to life again. The use of this verb indicates that Jesus was giving the Spirit in order to bring forth life, a new creation; through His resurrection, He became a life-giving Spirit.

The phrase "receive the Holy Spirit" establishes that the Spirit entered and began to live in the disciples. The Holy Spirit was given to regenerate them, to make them new creatures in Christ. This receiving of life from the Spirit preceded both their receiving the authority of Jesus and their baptism in the Holy Ghost on the day of Pentecost.

Before this time, the disciples were technically true believers and followers of Jesus and were saved according to the old covenant provisions. Yet they were not regenerated in the full sense of the New Covenant. Not until this point did the disciples enter into the new covenant provisions based on Jesus' death and resurrection. It was also technically at this time, not at Pentecost, that the church was born. The spiritual birth of the first disciples and the birth of the church are one and the same. It is crucial to understand the Holy Spirit's ministry to God's people. The disciples received the Holy Spirit (i.e., they were indwelt and regenerated by the Holy Spirit) before the day of Pentecost, and the outpouring of the Spirit in Acts 2:4 was an experience occurring after their regeneration by the Spirit. The baptism in the Spirit, therefore, is a second distinct work of the Holy Spirit in believers.

All believers receive the Holy Spirit at the time of their regeneration, (remember, I had a witness before my baptism) and afterward must experience the baptism in the Holy Ghost for power to be Christ's witness. The baptism in the Holy Ghost is an operation of the Spirit, distinct and separate from His work of regeneration. Just as His sanctifying work is a distinct work complementing His regenerating work, so the baptism in the Holy Spirit complements the regenerating and sanctifying work of the Spirit.

Nonetheless, the baptism of the Holy Spirit is closely linked with the external manifestation of speaking in tongues; it results in personal boldness and power to accomplish mighty works for Christ and to witness effectively, other results are prophetic utterances and declaration of praise, enhanced sensitivity to sin that grieves the Holy Spirit, a greater seeking after righteousness and a deeper awareness of God's judgement against ungodliness, new visions, manifestations of various gifts, a greater desire to pray, deeper love and understanding of God's word, etc.

The baptism in the Holy Spirit is sustained by a believer's life of prayer, worship in the Spirit, and sanctification.

Note: However powerful the initial coming of the Holy Spirit on the believer may be, if this does not find expression in a life of prayer, witness, and holiness, the experience will soon become a fading glory. You cannot overemphasise the importance of prayer – praying in the Spirit. In all kinds of prayer; prayer for the saints, worshipping and praising God, prayer for the nations and families, prayers of thanksgiving, and petitions as the Spirit gives you utterance.

The same Ephesians 6:18 talked about praying for the saints. This is the kind of prayer that is moved by love, empathy, compassion, humility to God, and selflessness; it is proof of one's spiritual maturity in knowing God and His will. God finds you attractive and valuable; like Anna and Simeon in Luke 2, God found them useful, and He kept them alive to see the promised Messiah.

Moses understood this, and he always prayed for the Israelites, he never allowed their attitude towards him to change his disposition towards God. Moses was not just meek, but also full of compassion, no wonder God showed him mercy too, for the scripture says in PS 18:25 "With the merciful, thou wilt shew thyself merciful..., and blessed are the merciful; for they shall obtain mercy- Matthew 5:7.

Praying for others reveals the content of your heart towards others, only the merciful and compassionate can leave their issues to intercede on behalf of others. At some point, God told Job to pray for his friends (Job 42), however, humanly speaking, it was Job who needed the prayer more. God is concerned for our physical well-being, but it is more interesting that we have His nature/character.

One of the benefits that praying for others brings is that it gives us a sense of gratitude and thereby distracts us from what would have kept us in an anxious state. When you think about other people's problems, it makes yours look very little. We must continue to pray for each other, not allowing faction and dissension among us. In that way, we continue to march together in victory over the evil one, when we don't, we open doors for limitation, and we may not manifest or enjoy all that is given to us through Christ.

UNDERSTANDING HINDERANCES TO PRAYERS

IGNORANCE: by this, I mean spiritual blindness/carnality. Many believers have not yet discovered who and what they have in Christ, and so the devil robs them.

FACTIONS: this is a form of division within the congregation into selfish groups or cliques. This destroys the unity of the church and hinders prayer.

DISSENSIONS: this could be aroused by the introduction of divisive teachings not supported by God's word (Romans 16:17). When you look at the church of today, you'll see some level of confusion; that is the cause of different doctrines and beliefs, which brings separation among believers.

DISCORD: This could be a result of the struggle for superiority in the house of God, which is the opposite of what Christ expects from His followers. Some believers have left the divine mandate, all they are focused on is title and other selfish gain in the house of God.

DOUBT: The opposite of faith is doubt, which is aroused through fear and guilt. We learned that doubt can only be overcome through much intake of God's word and by prayer and fasting because it is a demonic influence.

PRIDE: No proud person (taking oneself better than another) can receive anything from God; you must be humble before God and man- Luke 18:11-14.

DISOBEDIENCE: This is one of the things that steals your confidence and access to God, (Isa 59:1-2) because as a child of God, when we disobey God's command – He wouldn't be excited about it. Of course, the enemy would use that opportunity to taunt the offender, unless when you genuinely turn to God in repentance

PRETENCE/EYE SERVICE: Read- Matthew 6:5-8.

UNFORGIVENESS: Blessed are the merciful, for they shall obtain mercy from God and their fellow men (Matthew 6:14-15). You must also come before God with a clear conscience and without a grudge.

INGRATITUDE: The Bible says that we should bring our petitions with thanksgiving. When you don't recognize what God has done, how can you recognize the new things you are asking for? Thanksgiving draws the attention of God to those needs or issues you overlooked, so thank Him.

Many things could hinder one's prayer. Learn to be conscious (alert) of your activities so that the devil will not use you against yourself. For instance:

1 Peter 3:7,12 (NIV)- Husbands, in the same way be considerate as you live with your wives, and treat them with respect as the weaker partner and as heirs with you of the gracious gift of life, so that nothing will hinder your prayers. For the eyes of the Lord are on the righteous and His ears

are attentive to their prayer, but the face of the Lord is against those who do evil.

12

PRAY ALSO

Pray also for, that whenever I opened my mouth, words may be given me so that I will fearlessly make known the mystery of the gospel (Ephesians 6: 19). This is one way to annul the agenda of the devil here on earth, for whenever the Gospel is preached with great confidence and power, the world is touched by it.

Prayer is an aggressive weapon that puts the enemy in his place. A praying church is a powerful church, and nothing can be insurmountable for them. As you pray for yourself, remember God's work, pray for the servants of God, the missionaries across the globe, and the saints, it does avail much.

At one time, Jesus needed the prayers of others; He sought for His disciples to keep watch with Him. Remember, – iron sharpens iron, we all need each other, and we must be as one body in Christ, for united we stand, divided we fall.

Proverb 6:9- 10 – 9 How long will you lie there, you sluggard? When will you get up from your sleep? A little sleep, a little slumber, a little folding of hands to rest- and poverty will come on you like a bandit and scarcity like an armed man.

A sluggard or lazy person is one who puts off beginning what he or she should do, does not finish what has been started, and follows the least difficult course of action.

Slothfulness is even more tempting in the spiritual realm than it is in the physical. God exhorts us to make our calling and election sure with all eagerness. So, the church must rise from slumber and work out our salvation with fear, trembling, and all eagerness with every instrument God has fashioned for us.

CONCLUSION

The loss of the evil one is that you are prepared and cannot be seen off-guard, and each time he tries- he would be terrified at the level of your readiness. Our heavenly Father has enriched us with everything we could ever need. All we ought to do is know and utilise them, paying close attention to every detail and putting our complete trust in Him with the assurance that He does not disappoint those who build their worlds on His word (Luke 6:46-49). Key into the supernatural and see the wonders of God.

As a soldier of the cross, it is an essential requirement that you fortify yourself against the evil one. In addition, every victory starts with the mind, you must develop your mind-set to that of a winner. If you have a pessimistic mind-set- no matter how much of God's word you know, it could be unfruitful. What you know, which includes what you've learned from this book, is not for just memorising, you must receive it by faith for as many that believe and receive Him, are given power to walk in the supernatural. Develop your mental capacity, you can build a strong army for God only through your mind.

Always remember that the devil never quits, he goes to and fro (visiting the same place he had visited) seeking opportunity or loophole to carry out his desires, therefore, there's a charge to always be clothed with this complete garment. It is not a mistake that you are reading or have read this book because God orchestrates everything that happens in human life.

Plus, He desires that everyone knows and embraces His love and kindness. In case you have issues to settle with your maker you are not proud of your ways and relationship with God, and you know that somehow the devil is taking advantage of you, and you seek to be a better version of yourself; or maybe you see that there are areas of your life that this inspirational book has addressed and you need God to fix you so that you can begin to lead a victorious life full of God's presence, love, power and wisdom – just turn to God in prayer, He is right here with you and is attentive to your heart cry... Talk to him in prayer now.

He loves you, cares for your well-being and wishes to establish a covenant of peace with you. PRAY WITH ME...

Dear Lord Jesus,

I am not proud of the way I live my life; I am a sinner. But I want to become better for you, I am willing to embrace the love and all that you have given me. Please, Lord, forgive me and accept me as yours, I repent of all my sins today. Please deliver me from the power of sin and its guilt and restore my soul. I believe in my heart and I confess with my mouth that you are my Lord and Saviour, and I believe that God raised you from the dead. From today on, I declare that you're my Lord and Saviour. Thank you for paying the prize for me at the cross. Uphold me with your love, let your spirit come and dwell in me permanently; and disentangle me from every satanic bondage and relationship, I receive the grace and power to live a victorious Christian life, thank you, Lord Jesus Amen!

Congratulations if you just said that prayer, God has begun a new history of success for you and has given you a brand new life in Christ. Join any Bible-believing church around you and make yourself relevant to God, contact me at okoroaforcomfort2000@gmail.com

Have you read THE JEWEL OF GLORY?

It is entirely on a different level, It speaks on how God chooses His vessels and some of the processes it could take to make one into a masterpiece. This book serves as a guide to knowing the stages you're in as a believer or as a potential believer. To order, check out our contact

SOLUTION MANUAL FOR
CLASSICAL MECHANICS AND ELECTRODYNAMICS

Second Edition